Dreamquest

●

NATIVE AMERICAN MYTH
AND THE RECOVERY OF
SOUL

MORTON T. KELSEY

ELEMENT
Rockport, Massachusetts ● Shaftesbury, Dorset

© 1992 Morton T. Kelsey

Published in the U.S.A. in 1992 by
Element, Inc.
42 Broadway, Rockport, MA 01966

Published in Great Britain in 1992 by
Element Books Limited
Longmead, Shaftesbury, Dorset

The frontispiece is a depiction of the Seneca Creation Myth
as shown in Paul A. Wallace's *Indians in Pennsylvania*
(Harrisburg: the Pennsylvania Historical and Museum
Commission, 1991).
Designed by Roger Lightfoot
Cover illustration by Antowine Warrior
Cover designed by Max Fairbrother
Phototypeset by Intype, London
Printed and bound in the U.S.A. by
Edwards Brothers, Inc.

Library of Congress Cataloging-in-Publication Data

Kelsey, Morton T.
    Dreamquest : Native American myth and the recovery of soul /
Morton T. Kelsey.
    1. Spiritual life–Anglican authors. 2. Seneca Indians–Religion
and mythology. 3. Indians of North America–New York
(State)—Religion and mythology. I. Title.
BV4501.2.K42675 1992
299'.72–dc20   92–9594

British Library Cataloguing in Publication Data available

ISBN 1–85230–279–8

Contents

This book is dedicated to the memory
of Myra Etta Trippe Kelsey
who recorded these legends and saved them
for a later time.

A Remarkable Discovery

Everyone sat in rapt attention until the story ended. A period of quiet followed and then the listeners asked questions and pointed out details that had not been mentioned. Then they clamored for another story.

These stories were told from memory and very seldom were any details left out. Those who had heard them before would have objected had any phrase been omitted. The group ranged in age from three years to thirteen. In the winter we sat on the buffalo rug in front of the blazing fireplace and listened to the stories. On hot summer days we sat clustered around the swinging sofa on the front porch. The stories were told just as my mother first heard them, from memory. Grandfather's Seneca interpreter had told my mother many of them.

These stories had moved my mother so deeply that she wanted to record them, and so she went into the Allegany Reservation during a summer vacation from college in 1901. She took Grandfather's horse and buggy and a Seneca friend with her. Laboriously she wrote down these stories in longhand as an old Seneca woman told them. My mother spent most of the summer recording them.

I do not remember a time when I did not know these legends. They were part of the fabric of my childhood. I did not know why I was so drawn to them or why my friends wanted to hear them over and over again. I knew that they were Indian stories and knew that both of my parents had grown up in Salamanca, a small city built on land leased from the Seneca nation. The

Seneca people were one of the five nations of the Iroquois League. I knew that both of my deceased grandfathers had worked with and for the Seneca community and were outraged at the way land-hungry settlers and their government had lied, cheated, stolen Native American land, and broken treaty after treaty.

I remember clearly the trips we made in our open Buick touring car from eastern Pennsylvania to the Allegany Reservation in western New York, a real adventure in 1922. I knew that my father's family had purchased land taken from the Indians through duplicity by the Holland Land Company. In the first years of the nineteenth century, these pioneers had lumbered their land, created pastures and farm plots, and built houses.

One story I remember, apocryphal or not, was that the Senecas had been offered a reservation of either forty square miles or forty miles square, and not realizing the difference, they had chosen the former. The reservation lay a half mile on either side of the Allegany River. And then there was the "walking purchase," which meant that the amount of land that a man could walk around in one day was to be sold by the Iroquois. The whites stationed relay runners to ensure securing the largest possible area of land.

The treatment of the Native Americans lay heavy on my mother's heart. She continued her close association with the Senecas, was ritually adopted into one of the eight Seneca clans, and given an Indian name. Throughout the first third of the twentieth century, when few people were concerned about our treatment of the original people of North America, my mother spoke to gatherings all over Pennsylvania about their plight.

So long as my mother's Seneca friends were writing about their legends and myths, she did not wish to infringe on their rights. After she died in 1938, I kept a copy of these stories, which had been typed from her handwritten manuscript. As my children grew, I read these fascinating hero myths to them and they enjoyed them nearly as much as I had. I had not memorized them and something is lost when a story is read rather than told; it no longer seems to spring from the depth of the soul.

In the nineteen seventies, I decided I wanted these stories to reach a larger audience. My mother's Native American friends had died. I checked with experts in Seneca folklore at the State University of New York. No record of these legends could be found in any of the voluminous literature on the Seneca. The Seneca scholars found on record parts of only one story, but assured me that these legends were pure Seneca in names and attitudes. I decided that these stories should not be lost and with the help of Dove Publications in Pecos, New Mexico, they were printed and finally sold out. The publishing of these stories was a memorial to my mother, Myra Trippe Kelsey, who had preserved them.

However, I still saw them mainly as children's stories, tales that I had been told as a child, stories that took me into another world in a way that the Bible stories that were read to me did not do.

As well as I knew these stories, I never looked at them in the light of their primordial depth until my friend and editor, Richard Payne, suggested bringing them back into print along with a commentary to reveal the rich, universal symbols, images, and myths contained in this Seneca folklore. I read them again very slowly and carefully and was amazed to find that the rich vein of hero myth in them stirred me as much as it had when I was a child. With this impetus, I read these stories from a new perspective; they were no longer only the quaint and fascinating tales of my personal heritage. They were the hero myths of one of the most powerful, advanced, and enduring Native American peoples. They were stories of the human struggle with evil, of the pathway that leads to victory rather than defeat. They spoke of a spiritual dimension from which comes our power to do significant good or evil. They presented me with an enchanted primordial world in which spiritual reality and physical reality could not be separated, a unitary world in which these two dimensions met and intermingled.

These stories gave me a picture not only of the Seneca Nation of the Iroquois, but of the depth of my own being, the primal level of our humanness. They spoke of my struggles and conflicts, my pain and victory, how I might win victory over evil; they spoke of the universal struggle of human beings to survive, the struggle of the hero to overcome obstacles and to achieve victory, to defeat the powers that would destroy us. The hero was the one who knew how to call upon powers greater than human — spiritual, divine, creative, helpful realities. The stories also spoke of spiritual evil and of human beings who are possessed by these evil powers, or who call upon them. Witches, both men and women, were very real to the Iroquois. The hero had to have human courage and endurance, but he also needed to be in touch with powers from beyond the human level, powers that could defeat those beings who sought to do mischief and were in the service of evil.

Frank Baum's stories of Oz gave me a similar picture of good and evil witches and the hero's way. As a child I received a little book about the Greek heroes and was fascinated as I read how Perseus, Theseus, Hercules, and Jason struggled to overcome seemingly impossible odds and horrible, vicious creatures because they were given divine direction and help. *The Arabian Nights' Entertainments* held a similar attraction for me. All these stories were a tremendous inspiration in my sickly and handicapped childhood. These heroes showed that it was possible to win in spite of great difficulties if one had divine guidance and help. Life was filled with malignant realities and obstacles, but one need not be overcome by them. I recently realized that Beethoven also struggled to overcome suffering, deafness, and rejection and left the record of his victory in his late music. The hero's way is a universal way and is open to all.

During the last fifty years, I have been immersed by my inner necessity in the depth and complexity of the human soul. I found that much present-day theology and biblical study were not enough. Although the Bible is filled with heroes — Abraham, Joseph, Moses, Gideon, Jepthah, Elijah, Elisha and the prophets — they were not portrayed to me as figures that I could follow and imitate.

Even in my years at seminary I was not given the idea that the Holy Spirit and the risen Jesus were realities upon which I could call to help me survive and grow. The teachings of Jesus and the early Church made clear that evil was real and was still operative in the world, both through and in spite of human beings. This reality was not taken seriously in modern religious thought. Equally neglected was the idea that we could be heroes as we called upon the Spirit and reality of the risen Christ and overcame the evil that is so much a part of our broken world.

As I studied depth psychology I realized that there were psychologists who believed that we are in touch with both physical and spiritual realms. I began to record and study my dreams. I found that I needed help to understand them and the dreams of others who came to me to talk about their spiritual concerns and difficulties. I discovered in my dreams the same images and symbols that I had found in these Native American hero stories and in Greek, Norse, and Arabian mythology. Indeed, the stories of the Old and New Testaments came to life for me in a new way.

Wherever I have traveled I have found the same symbols and beliefs, the same concerns with the ambivalent spiritual dimension and its effect upon our ordinary material existence. The Australian Aborigines call this dimension the Dream World. The indigenous religion of China is clearly aware of malicious spiritual powers and seeks to avoid them. The Senoi of Malaysia (related to the Australian Aborigines) believe that dreams reveal the depth of the soul and the soul's contact with another dimension of reality; the Senoi discuss their dreams with one another over breakfast. European fairytales or folktales speak the same symbolic language. I will never forget entering the Forbidden City in Beijing and seeing before me two huge bronze turtles guarding the entrance to one of its most important buildings. Here were the very same turtles of which I had dreamed in a very significant dream, figures that had opened me to a whole new world of fantasy.

These Sencca legends reveal the universal nature of the human soul or psyche and the total world in which it lives. And they may reveal more of the vast world with which we are in touch than even our personal dreams do. Indeed, it is nearly impossible to interpret our dreams without a knowledge of the images and symbols of mythology and folklore. And seldom do we take our dreams seriously until we see in them the boundless panorama of symbolic reality. When these hero stories are understood, they can give us a pictorial anatomy of the human soul and the limitless worlds with which it is in contact.

Thirty-five years ago I came to a crossroad. I had been deeply influenced by depth psychology and equally by the theology of Baron von Hügel. I was studying psychology in Zurich, Switzerland. Instead of any hint that I should become a secular psychologist, I repeatedly dreamed of building Byzantine churches. As I looked more and more deeply into Eastern Orthodox Christianity and at the symbolism of the Greek and Russian Icon, I realized that this branch of Christianity had never lost its belief that the Holy still touches this world in dreams, visions, and healing. These Christians believed in the depth of the soul and its capacity to be touched and transformed by the Divine. I needed to have a theological point of view that undergirded that belief, and at the same time, a systematic psychology that enabled us to be heroes, instruments of the Holy. I realized that Western Christianity needed both a religious psychology and a psychological theology.

I was much moved many years ago when I read Joseph Campbell's *The Hero with a Thousand Faces*. Human beings needed and were looking for a savior who could empower them. I was deeply touched by C.S. Lewis' stories of Narnia, by Tolkien's epic about hobbits, and Madeleine L'Engle's magnificent children's stories. The profound and mysterious myths in Charles Williams' seven novels brought me closer to the essential meaning of Christianity than most works of theology had. As I reflected on these Seneca legends, I realized that they had laid a foundation for an understanding of a strange and hopeful world in which we actually live, a world that is a mysterious intermingling of matter and spirit. I explored the depth of meaning in these legends and saw why they had made such an impression on me, both as a child and an adult. Then I wanted to share with others what I had discovered in these profound stories.

CHAPTER ONE

The Images, Symbols, and Myths of the Iroquois

The folklore of any people reveals not only the universal, primal depth of the human psyche, but also the distinguishing and unique characteristics of a people, culture, or nation. In his discussion of the tragedy of Nazism, C.G. Jung points out the fatal and hypnotic power of the old Teutonic war god, Wotan. He also notes that the myth that Wagner dramatized in his magnificent *Der Ring des Nibelungen* ends with the total destruction of human beings, the gods, and even heaven itself. He suggests that this myth explains something of both the power and disaster of Nazism.

I knew in my bones something about the Seneca and the Iroquois through their stories, through my mother's deerskin dress and her beaded clan insignia, and through the stories of both of my grandmothers. I realized that I needed to know much better the history, culture, and mythology of Six Nations and of the Seneca in particular if I were adequately to interpret these legends. I already knew the depth of the human psyche and its primal religious striving to deal with total reality.

In a recent interview, Wendy Doniger, the University of Chicago authority on mythology, put this viewpoint clearly. She said that anthologists now discuss myth as the product of a human being of a particular time who lived in a certain region, ate a particular food, and lived according to distinctive customs. The same knowledge is necessary for significant dream interpretation. Although we can find many primal, archetypal images in the dreams of ordinary people, we need to know the history and background of each individual if we are to adequately interpret his or her dreams.

In order to get this information about the Senecas, I immediately called my cousin, Helen Landon, who still lived in the house that my grandfather had built in Salamanca on the Seneca Allegany Reservation. She sent me package after package of books relating to the Seneca people. By good fortune I also met Huston Smith through an old friend, Phil Novak, who is a professor of World Religions at the Dominican College in the San Francisco area. The latter provided me with a magnificent bibliography on Native American culture. For several months I immersed myself in the history and culture of the Iroquois and the Seneca people. I found *The Death and Rebirth of the Seneca* by Anthony F.C. Wallace the most detailed and comprehensive study available. I was amazed at the wealth of available material relating to the Iroquois Nations.

I found that these people had been one of the most significant influences in the development of North America. They were sophisticated survivors who still held onto their culture and religion despite three hundred and fifty years of European attempts to destroy it. They were the only Native Americans east of Mississippi who still held any of their ancestral lands. Their ancient religion was still practiced, their political wisdom had influenced the American form of government, and they still considered themselves a sovereign nation. The religions of the Incas, Mayas, and Aztecs have survived only in historical documents and monumental buildings; the Seneca way of life still lived on.

Before we look in greater detail at the history and culture of the Seneca, we need to understand more about the primal religion the Native American people and the Iroquois shared. In his totally rewritten classic study of human religion, now entitled *The World's Religions*, Huston Smith has inserted a chapter on primal religion. He allowed me to see his proof copy. He points out that in most Native American languages there is no word for "art." Everything these people did was religious as well as art or hunting or dance or cultivating a garden. It is possible to learn about the religion of a people by observing hunters preparing for the hunt, women tilling the ground and tending their squash and maize and beans, warriors getting ready for war, people performing their ritualistic dances, or painting and sculpting their masks, as well as in the design of the buildings in which they lived. Even the utensils used for cooking had "religious" meaning. The following stories also reveal the nature of these peoples' daily lives, their culture, religion, and the unitary quality of their existence.

My wife and I have experienced the unitary quality of primal religions in many places. In 1948, we were traveling through northern Arizona and witnessed the Hopi Snake Dance. In it, children of ten and men in their eighties handled live rattlesnakes in a complex dance asking for rain. After the dance, torrential rains poured down on us so that we were nearly mired in the muddy roads. We found the same combination of social gathering, feasting, and elaborate, exquisite dancing among the Hupa and Yurok tribes of northern California at the White Deerskin Dance. In Bali we found the same merging of the secular and the sacred in the colorful community presentations of portions of their sacred epic, the *Ramayana*. This event was a religious celebration, a magnificent dramatic event, a community gathering, and a tourist attraction all in one. In Malaysia on the grounds of a five-star hotel we discovered a well-kept little shrine where daily offerings were made to placate the spirit of a ghost who was bothering people in that neighborhood. (This shrine was not maintained for tourists!)

Every Chinese or Hindu home, hotel, or restaurant that we visited prominently displayed a lighted shrine with offerings to the spirits. In Transkei in South Africa, the Zionist Christians see themselves as the new Zion. One finds there a vital religious life and the inseparable quality of a spiritual-material world, a sacramental view of reality. Jung reminds us that once we get a safe distance from Western Europe and those cultures that sprang from it we find little separation between the sacred and the profane.

When Wendy Doniger was asked what has caused the great new interest in mythology, she replied that few of our churches are providing the symbolic food human beings need for survival. Contemporary women and men are not adequately nourished on a diet of reason, logic, and matter alone. When I was a child, the Seneca legends gave me an entrance into an enchanted land. Rereading them again brought me face-to-face with the universal symbols of death and resurrection, of good and evil, of the persistent reality of spirit, and of the way of the hero, who is able to triumph over obstacles and even evil itself.

One European psychiatrist observed that patients from North America had dreams and fantasies different from those of his European patients. We North Americans may have been more influenced by the native American culture than we realize. Perhaps we are closer to the primal images than we think.

THE WISE, ENDURING, AND INFLUENTIAL IROQUOIS

Nearly all educated people are impressed by the tremendous culture that developed and flowered in the American continents before the coming of the Europeans. Magnificent cities and buildings have been excavated in Central America. Several different cultures flourished in Mexico, and the astounding Mayan remains are scattered through many Central American countries. The Spanish conquerors could hardly believe the sophistication, wealth, and detailed social organization of the Inca Empire they conquered and destroyed. Most of these nations were led by omnipotent rulers, and in these cultures individual human life had little value.

In the fertile woodlands of northeastern North America, a different kind of civilization appeared, a democratic federation called the Iroquois League consisting of five, self-ruling nations. Their leaders met to keep the peace and to solve all important matters between them and between them and other peoples. A sixth nation, the Tuscarora, joined the federation later.

This group of equal nations among equals was one of the first attempts known in history at this kind of living. In addition, this society, centered in the fertile valleys of New York State, reached out through alliances, from the Mississippi to the Atlantic coast, and stretched from North Carolina to the Great Lakes and into Canada. One of the most important reasons that I am writing these words in English rather than in French is that the

French, under the direction of Samuel de Champlain, attacked several Iroquois villages in 1615 and won the undying hatred of the Iroquois. When France and England were struggling over domination of the North American continent, the Iroquois League sided with the British. One of the tragedies of the American Revolution resulted from the splitting of the League; the Senecas, Cayuga, Onondoga, and Mohawks sided with the British, the Tuscarora and the Oneida with the American Revolution.

The colonial frontier at that time stretched from just west of the Hudson River south into the Carolinas. During the Revolution, the Native Americans and their British allies pursued a "scorched earth" policy of killing and destruction which started the "bad and savage Indian" stereotype that has dogged the heels of most Native North Americans ever since. From the Natives' point of view, they were simply protecting their own country from the incursions of a violent and trigger-happy frontier people.

The breaking of treaties and the shabby way these Indian Nations were treated after the Revolution is too well known to be told again. The magnificent heartland of the Iroquois that was left to them melted away before their eyes; they were tricked into selling it under the influence of alcohol and bribes to a group of Dutch bankers who called themselves the Holland Land Company. The Native Americans still living in and around the reservations had little way to make a living. The confederacy collapsed and this once proud people was reduced to living in wilderness slums.

And then a miracle occurred and the nation was reborn. One of the leaders of the Senecas, Handsome Lake, after more than thirty years of violence and debauchery, was at the point of death. His family was called to be with him. He woke out of this near-death experience and told those around him that he had experienced a shamanistic journey on the strawberry road into the presence of the creator. There he was told that he was to preach the old religion and call people to repentance for not following it and for indulging in four vices: whiskey, witchcraft, love-magic, and abortion (and sterility medicine). Two other major visions occurred and a renewed Native American religion emerged.

A Quaker, Henry Simmons, was present at the first vision and observed the transformation of the Seneca Nation. Handsome Lake traveled through the remains of the Six Nations preaching repentance and renewal. Simmons commented that those who followed the new-old religion appeared to be solid and weighty in spirit and that he felt "the love of God flowing powerfully among us."

To this day one can visit one of the Iroquois longhouses and hear the entire story of the visions of Handsome Lake recited from memory and share in their religious and social festivities; these are still not separate. Most of the traditional rituals are still practiced, the mid-winter festival, the flowing of the maple sap thanksgiving, the corn planting ceremony, the strawberry festival (according to tradition, the road to heaven is lined with ripe strawberries and is called the strawberry road), the harvest thanksgiving, and the White Dog ceremony (now slightly altered from its original form). The depth of religious life is still there.

The Iroquois Nations are quite alive. Since the Iroquois see themselves as a sovereign nation, they issue passports that are honored by many countries. Recently some of the leaders of the council of sachems, the peace council of the Iroquois, were invited to Bogota, Colombia, in support of a tribe of Meskita Natives in Nicaragua who were rebelling against the government and were equally hostile to the Contras. They traveled on their Iroquois passports. Their peacemaking efforts have a long history that begins in the shadowy world where myth and history meet and intermingle.

The confederacy began with the transformation of Hiawatha (not to be confused with Longfellow's hero). The many different tribes of the Iroquois had been at war with each other; chaos prevailed among the Five Nations. At last Hiawatha, depressed by the death of his children and his wife, disappeared into the forest where he preyed upon travelers, killing and eating them. (We shall find evidences in the following legends of people who were called "man-eaters" or cannibals. They were treated with scorn and sometimes considered witches.)

One day the Peacemaker, a god named Dekanawidah, came

across the lakes in a stone canoe and appeared to Hiawatha. This was a moment of transformation such as was experienced by Handsome Lake many centuries later. Hiawatha realized the horror of his cannibalism and of the war and chaos among his people. He started on a mission of peace as representative of the Peacemaker. His transformation and his eloquence soon converted all the chiefs of the original Five Nations and the remarkable Confederacy of the Iroquois was founded in which payments were substituted for blood feuds. War was not to be undertaken except by the unanimous vote of the Grand Council, made up of chiefs of each of the Nations. Some anthropologists date the founding of the League one or two hundred years before the coming of the Europeans in 1600; the Iroquois place it a thousand years before that time.

The Iroquois have sometimes been referred to as the Greeks among the Native Americans. But even the Greeks were never able to come up with such a creative social solution to their wars, and Greek society was based upon slave labor and was one in which women had little worth. The Six Nations held women in great esteem. The society was a fascinating marriage of a matrilineal society, where family names were passed through the woman's line, and a patriarchal system, where the men were the hunters, warriors, and protectors of the community. The women did the farming of the staple foods maize, corn, beans, and squash.

Although the chiefs of each village were ostensibly men, they could be deposed by a council of women. Most of the captives from outside the Six Nations were not treated as slaves, but were adopted into families. Such a political/social structure has not often been tried among human beings.

Those who drew up the Constitution of the United States may have been influenced by the model presented by the Six Nations of Iroquois. Both Benjamin Franklin and James Madison were familiar with the functioning of the Iroquois confederacy and deeply impressed with it; they felt they could and should do as well. At one time consideration was given to calling the legislative arm of the new government of the United States the Grand Council, in Iroquois fashion.

The influence of the Six Nations Confederacy made a real

impact upon European thought as well through the writings of John Locke and Jean-Jacques Rousseau who spoke of the noble "savage" and their principles of human freedom. Their writings helped ignite revolutions throughout the Western world, a major move from autocratic government. In 1851, Lewis Henry Morgan wrote *League of the Iroquois*, one of the first serious studies of a nonwestern ethnic group. This book fell into the hands of Friedrich Engels, who was Karl Marx's close associate. The positive picture of this League did much in shaping Engel's later thinking and that of Lenin. The Iroquois experiments with freedom and peace have had an incalculable effect upon our Western world.

THE IROQUOIS VISION OF REALITY

When human beings talk about the ultimate nature of reality, they usually resort to pictures and stories. In just the same way, logical thinking breaks down when physicists try to describe the ultimate nature of light or matter; it also fails when we try to describe the ultimate meaning and nature of the world in which we live. We have already noted the pessimistic Teutonic religion. The popular modern myth or picture of reality describes our universe as the meaningless, chaotic, and random product of interacting meaningless bits of matter. This picture gives little meaning to human life or suffering. There is also the opposite myth that only soul and spirit are real and matter is an illusion. The Greeks' myth of creation told of many ambivalent gods who were often in conflict with one another. None of these views gives much understanding or acknowledgment of the reality of human destiny or human suffering.

The Persians' view of the universe was of a god of light struggling against a god of evil and darkness. Light needed human help to win the struggle. The Gnostic myth perceives the creation of the present world as a catastrophe in which divine reality fell into the clutches of useless, vile, and evil matter that became the prison house of the soul. Most physical pleasures were therefore considered dangerous, something to be rejected. Some Christian practice has been influenced by this view. Still another view told stories about a good creative spiritual power that made the world good; but something went wrong and evil, misery, sickness, and death broke into creation to plague human beings and to interfere with their destiny.

The myths of the Seneca and Iroquois peoples, as well as those of many other Native North Americans, tell of an essentially benign deity who wanted to help human beings, but something went wrong. The people needed to call upon this deity's caring power by rituals and proper living in order to avoid the disasters which sometimes struck down the best of human beings. The Christian story of the fall and redemption from it is similar in many ways to the Seneca myth. The visions of Handsome Lake present this view dramatically and so did the Seneca creation stories. In many ways, the Iroquois creation and hero myths are more humane and hopeful than those of the Greeks. The latter had both a written language and the superb poets, Homer and Hesiod, to describe them. Thus, the myths they told have had an incalculable influence on European thought and literature. The Native Americans who still follow the new-old way of Handsome Lake hear their myths recited from memory, just as the Greek myths were before they were recorded in written form.

Let's listen to the story of creation in its Seneca version. These myths will give us the framework for understanding the primal depth of the hero legends that follow.[1]

THE SENECA CREATION MYTH

Before the earth existed, a human-like sky people lived in a realm of complete beauty, comfort, and fruitfulness. Neither sun nor moon nor stars existed. Light was given by a great tree that grew in this realm. The same tree produced darkness at night. Every need was provided for in this sky world and no one had to work. It was a heavenly Garden of Eden.

Living in this world was a family who had five sons. The youngest of them developed a passionate love for a young woman and grew very sick. His parents went to her and she consented to become his wife. He soon recovered, but shortly afterwards fell sick again and grew weaker and weaker. He finally called his oldest brother and told him of a dream that revealed what he must do in order to recover. He had dreamed that his youngest brother said to him, "The living tree, The-Tree-That-Is-Called-Tooth, must be pulled out by the hands of your four brothers or you will die." He also dreamed that the tree had spoken to him saying, "There is another generation coming out of the living tree. It will sprout out of the ground beside the living tree that gives light and all the blessings of our world."

The brothers understood, but were fearful and complained that it would mean the end of their world, but the youngest brother told them that a new tree would grow up beside the old one. The old tree was to be the source of the creation of a solid world in which it would be rooted and live forever. The brothers argued with the sick one until he said, "It is a true dream that has power by itself. It must be done; if not, I shall die because of my disobedience." Each of the four brothers tried to pull down the tree, but only the youngest was able to tear it loose. As he did, the whole tree, leaves and branches, trunk and roots, fell through a great hole in the sky.

The sick brother immediately grew stronger. He got up and called his wife and they went to see what had happened to the tree. They found only a great hole in the plain. He asked his wife to sit next to him and she came. He blessed the tree that fell through the hole and the tree that remained. While they sat by the hole and gazed at the light below, a breath of air came up through the hole. It was the gentle south wind, the breath of life; from this air she conceived a child. Her husband told her to look at the light below and then told her that this was to be her new home and that she would be the mother of earth-beings. Then he pushed her and she fell through the hole in the sky.

At first she was not anxious or fearful; she truly believed that she would indeed be mother to a new kind of people. But she fell a very long time. As she looked from where she came, she could not see the hole, only the blue sky. A white bird flew by her and asked her if she was frightened, and she said that she was. The bird then became a human being who told her that she would be helped and would find a place to live upon the great waters below. Another being came and told her, "You will see tens of thousands of creatures of the air and of the water below. They are preparing to care for you." As she came close to the water, a vast flock of birds flew up to her and cushioned her fall.

A great council of all the animals of air and water gathered to find which of them would be able to support her in the water. However, every one of them refused to help except for a mud turtle who said, "I never tire out or die without my father's consent." Mud Turtle swam up to the surface of the water and the woman rested upon his back; the birds rested there, too.

The turtle grew very quickly. All the creatures of water and sky searched for bits of earth and ground. Soon they had created an earth large enough for her to walk around. The mud turtle then told her, "I will stand forever under you, for you to live upon. A great race will come from you and build upon the earth, for it was given to me to have the power to do this and it shall be fulfilled according to a dream from above. I shall stand under the earth until the Great Spirit calls for me." All the animals on earth rejoiced to have a place to rest and they praised Mud Turtle, who was their foundation.

Soon after the woman was established on the new earth she gave birth to a little girl. She called her "daughter." In a very short time the daughter could talk. Then she was able to stand and walk around. When she was large enough to go out of their home, she loved to go outside and play in the water. Her mother told her that she must not go into the water. When she became a young woman she disobeyed her mother, and went into the water to play and swim. Soon after this her mother found that she was pregnant, and her mother knew that she had conceived by going into the water and was carrying the child of the spirit of the great deep.

The daughter was bearing twins within her, the Good Spirit, Tarachiawagon, and the Evil Twin, Tawiskaron. Even before birth the brothers quarreled. The one said, "Let us be born the natural way and save our mother." The other one said, "Let us go out the nearest and quickest way." The Good Twin came out as children naturally do, but the other said, "I will go out the nearest way and the cleanest way because I can see the light under her left arm." The Evil Twin was born in that way.

The woman knew that she was dying and called to her mother and told her how she wanted to be buried. The mother took her body and buried it in the ground and laid her head to the wind. Ten days later corn sprouted from her breasts. The mother took the corn and planted it to provide food for the earth dwellers who would live there forever.

The grandmother of the children took them after she had buried her daughter. She found that they were healthy. Then it became dark and she went to sleep. When she awoke it was light and she heard the twins talking to each other. The Good Spirit said, "Let the sun be created and rise against the wind, and make light." And it was so. Then he created the moon to give light at night. His brother made fun of him for creating good things.

The Good Spirit created a man out of the dust of the earth and breathed the breath of life into him, and he became a living soul. The Good Spirit tried to create vegetables and plants, but they did not grow because he had not created the rain and because there was no woman to till the soil and multiply the earth. So the Good Spirit then created rain and a woman. He brought the man and woman together and told them that they were husband and wife, then he told them, "And you shall enjoy yourselves upon the earth in order to multiply from generation to generation. And here are vegetables and herbs to sustain life from the fruits of the earth, which shall grow forever."

Then the Good Twin created rivers with double currents so that you could always paddle downstream. He improved the corn that grew from his mother's grave and created all the animals that were good to eat, including deer, elk, and bear.

The Evil Spirit tagged after him and made evil things, monsters, reptiles, worms, frogs, and bats. He made the streams to flow only one way and put in rapids and waterfalls. He sent blights to the corn and made caves, storms, sickness, and death.

When his work was finished, the Good Spirit walked over the earth to look at his creation. Far to the west on the rocky rim of the world he met his brother disguised as a great giant;

he could take many forms. He asked this stranger, as he asked all those he met, what he was doing. The giant said, "Looking over my creation." The Good Spirit said with emphasis, "It is *my* creation," They violently disagreed. They decided to settle their argument by a contest of power. The one who could move the rocky mountains the greatest distance would win. The Evil Spirit moved them only a few feet. Then the Good Spirit made the giant turn with his back to the mountains. He moved the mountains many miles, right up behind the giant, and told him to turn around. The giant turned and smashed his nose into the mountain.

Then the giant made known who he was and said, "You are the Creator. I submit and beg to be allowed to live." The request was granted if, and only if, the Evil Spirit would help the people and take them as his grandchildren. So the pact was made between them. If the people would make and wear masks representing this now ambivalent being and would burn tobacco for him and give him a little cornmeal, he would give them power to withstand the cold of winter, to drive away sickness, destructive winds, witches, and even to handle hot coals without being burned.

Masks known as The Faces, False Faces, or Giant-False-Faces represented the evil power that had been tamed by the Creator, the Good Spirit. They were an essential part of Iroquois life. The twisted noses of many of the masks were a remembrance, or more truly, a sacramental sign, an icon of the Evil Spirit's defeat. The masks were carved, most often from the soft wood of a living basswood tree. These Faces represented the Evil Spirit itself, also any one of the legion of spirits known by all sorts of names related to the Giant Tamed Evil Spirit.

It is well to remember that the spirit of evil in Christianity has been known by a myriad of names, as Jeffrey Burton Russell has shown in his monumental four-volume historical study of the idea of evil, *The Devil, Satan, Lucifer*, and *Mephistopheles*. The Iroquois and Seneca way of life was devoted to enjoying the earth and avoiding the evil that was so much a part of it. The real hero relied not on his or her own power, but was one who could avoid evil and knew how to be filled with the creative power of the spiritual dimension of reality. One could be a hero in war, in hunting, in wisdom, in knowing and presenting the rituals. The chief was to exemplify the hero as one who had a skin seven thumbs thick, untouched by malicious gossip and nasty criticism, who acted always in the best interest of all the people, not only those now alive, but of the generations yet to come, and who led a good, clean personal life.

In 1838, Blacksmith, a chief on the Tonawanda Reservation, told the following account of the origin of the Senecas and it was recorded for posterity:

> Traditionally the people known today as the Seneca originated from the top of a large hill called Ge-nun-de-wah-ga or the Great Hill — hence the name "The Great Hill People," or "People of Stone" for Seneca Indians. This hill is located at the head of Canandaigua Lake in central New York. After the Creator caused the original Senecas to be formed from the interior of the Great Hill, they emerged from a hole in the top and built their first village on it. They found that they were entirely encircled by a huge snake whose insatiable appetite and poisonous breath killed all those who attempted to escape. The head and tail of the snake met at a narrow path at the bottom of the hill that was the only exit.
>
> Over the years the Seneca people became overcrowded and approached starvation as a result of their confinement. Eventually they decided to attempt armed escape. All of the men, women, and children took up their arrows, clubs, and spears and descended the hill to battle the snake. It swallowed all members of the small tribe except two children who miraculously escaped.
>
> By means of an oracle (probably a dream), the Creator later instructed the two surviving children to make a willow bow and arrow tipped with a special poison with which to kill the serpent. Bravely the orphan children approached the snake and shot the arrow under the scales. Immediately the snake began to thrash violently about, uncoiling from around the hill, and as he vomited the skulls of the dead Senecas, these rolled down the side of the hill into the lake and immediately petrified. They are to be seen today at the bottom of the lake in the form of large, round stones. As the snake convulsed in its death throes, it rolled down the hillside uprooting trees in its path and creating a cleft in the hillside. Finally it fell into the water. The Seneca Indians sprang from these two heroic orphans.

HERO STORIES

As we read and listen to the hero stories that follow we hear many echoes of these myths, the same primal depth. These people lived in an enchanted world aware of little distinction between the spiritual and the physical. These stories reflect an ancient time. There is no mention of white people. Little reference is made to a time before the highly developed village life that the French found when they came in 1600. The stories speak of origins and of heroes with magical powers, of witches and dreams, of powers for good and evil that surrounded them. They come from the Allegany Reservation that one anthropologist called an island of antiquity. How long they were passed down by word of mouth no one can tell with certainty. They speak of the primal level that still exists within each of us.

Before I began to study these fascinating people I did not realize many of their most significant characteristics: the importance of dreams for these people; the fear they had of the spiritual power used in witchcraft; their abiding confidence in a benign spiritual reality; and their willingness to help one another through suffering and sorrow. As I read the stories with this background, I came to admire these heroic people, true survivors in a world hostile to them. I also found my confidence and hope in a transforming spiritual power reaffirmed and strengthened.

I have been recording my dreams for more than forty years. I have found them incredibly helpful, not only in dealing with my personal problems, but also in giving me access to the vast, ambivalent spiritual realm (what Jung calls the collective unconscious). When I found that most Christians have little interest in dreams, I did a careful study of the dreams mentioned in the Bible and in the history of the Christian Church. I discovered that the dream was seen not only as a means of knowing about ourselves, but was also perceived as one of the most common ways by which the Divine spoke to human beings. This was accepted by nearly all Christians until well into the seventeenth century in Western Europe and *still remains an essential part of the practice and belief of the Orthodox Churches.*[2] I have also studied other cultures and found that the dream is taken seriously in virtually all cultures that have not been contaminated by Western materialism. In all the cultures that I have examined, I have seen none, not even the well-known Senoi of Malaysia, for whom the dream was more central to life and culture than the Iroquois. Where dreams are revered, myths are also very important, and the spiritual world is seen as interpenetrating the physical realm and making itself known to ordinary human beings.

When the spiritual dimension of reality is perceived as part and parcel of ordinary life, ritual is also understood as being of great importance. Religious practice and ritual are the living and acting out of a mythical worldview. They are the socially acceptable, creative way to be touched by the benign aspects of spiritual reality.

However, when people believe in good and evil aspects of spirituality, we will usually find witchcraft — the personal and malicious use of evil spiritual powers to gain power for that particular individual. Witches were believed to wreak vengeance upon their enemies by using magical spells and rituals to cause sickness and disaster to other people, their animals, or crops. Among the Iroquois the punishment for witches was speedy death. Evidences of this punishment for those believed to be witches is found well into the early years of the nineteenth century. Before we are too quick to criticize, we need to remember that our European forebearers were still burning witches during the previous century. Witchcraft was part of Seneca culture, as we shall see in many of these mythical stories.

Another remarkable element of Iroquois culture is found in the treatment of women. When these hero legends were told, the Iroquois were probably just emerging from a matrilineal culture. Throughout these hero stories we often find women portrayed in a negative light. But women were never reduced to the position of chattel as they were in ancient Greece, the Near East, China, India, and in many places in Africa.[3]

Not only could the women's council depose a chief if he were inept, the women had their own rituals and dances which the whole community attended. One particular dance of very ancient flavor was a "woman's choice" in which the women selected their partners. It was also called the hand-holding dance.[4]

In most of the stories we find a boy living with his uncle. In matrilineal societies where impregnating men came and went, a woman's sons were usually raised by her brother, an ancient matrilineal practice. However, the first of our legends is about a father and son. The Iroquois were able to emerge from a society dominated by the Great Mother Goddess without reducing women to the level of slaves, but treated them nearly as peers, a unique testimony to their conciliatory nature, to say the least. They did not seem to have the morbid fear of women found in most patriarchal societies.

Myths, legends, fairytales, folktales, and dreams are made of the same images, symbols, pictures, signs, and characters. All across the world myths tell similar stories. How are we to understand them? Jung, in his article on the Trickster, and Marie-Louise von Franz in her book, *An Introduction to the Psychology of Fairytales*, suggest that like dreams these legends have a discernible structure, similar to that of longer dreams. First of all, they give us the time and place of the story. Then the actors in the drama are introduced. Sometimes other characters are added as the story unfolds. Then we are presented with the exposition of the story, the problem to be solved. Then follows the crisis and finally, the solution.

In the first story a boy is left with his sister and a dog, after his father goes to find his unfaithful wife. The development of the story follows the ups and downs in the hero's journey. Some of the stories go on and on, while others are relatively simple and short. And then comes the climax of the story in which the hero either finds success or disaster. Most of these Seneca myths portray a successful and benign hero. In many of the Greek and Teutonic stories, the conclusions are tragic indeed. The legend builds to this place of tension and disaster follows. In most of these stories, however, the one in danger is saved, the evil and malicious characters are destroyed, and the hero happily marries the maiden.

We now present an archetypal hero. Read the following story as you would any other and see what impact it makes on you. Then think of how it affected the Native American children and youths who listened on winter evenings by the fire pits of the longhouse as one of the old men or women told the story from memory. In the chapter that follows the story, we will present

our meditation and reflection on the symbols that emerge as the
hero makes his way to victory.

CHAPTER TWO

Da-ne-da-do

There was a man who lived in a house built of hemlock boughs. His name was Da-ne-da-do. He lived in the western part of the country, alone on a farm which he had cleared himself. He had no ax. When he wished to fell a tree, he would build a fire against it to make it fall. When the tree was felled, he burned the trunk and branches into lengths which could be handled easily. Where these fires burned, the ground was warmed. In these places he planted corn. Da-ne-da-do worked for many years until he had a wide space cleared. He had no plow or hoe. Each year he would put the corn into the same hills that he had used the year before. By planting corn year after year, he always had plenty of white and flint corn for hominy and corn bread.

He also needed meat. He did not have to use a gun or bow and arrow. He knew how to get meat another way. All Da-ne-da-do had to do was to walk over a path through the forest in a great circle leading back to his home. In the afternoon he walked over the path again. Every animal that stepped on his track died. He picked up these animals and carried them home to dress them. He was a rich man, for he had in his home several deerskin bottles full of bear's oil.

For many years, Da-ne-da-do lived alone. One day on returning from hunting, he found that a woman had come to his house. As soon as she saw him she said, "I came to marry you and live with you. Here are the wedding cakes."

She showed him a basket of corn cakes. They were made in a peculiar shape, long with round knobs at each end. He looked at them. He thought about it. Then he said, "We will live together."

After a while a boy was born. The family was happy and peaceful. Years passed. The boy grew to be eight years old. Then his sister was born. One morning before the little girl was two years old, her father went as usual to catch game. In the afternoon he went again. He expected to find game. He found none. He feared now that he had an enemy.

The next day he went out as usual in the morning. He went again in the afternoon. This day also he found nothing. Then he was sure he had an enemy. He had never before failed to bring home a deer or a bear, but the last two days he had caught nothing.

He thought a long time about it. When his wife went out to draw some water, Da-ne-da-do asked his son what mother did while father was away. The boy cried and said, "Mother forbade me to tell you anything."

The father said, "You must tell me."

The boy answered, "My mother will punish me if I tell you, but since you are my father, I think it is no more than right that I should tell you. When you are out of sight, mother throws me out of the door. She puts a pail out, too. I must get water. Mother says, "I am going to wash your sister; go away for a while." While I am gone she takes a bath herself. She puts on her best clothes and all her beads. She goes away. She always goes toward the south."

The boy did not finish his story, for his mother came in and went to work. After a while she went out again. As soon as she was gone the boy said, "Mother always gets back before you return. She takes off her beads right away, and when you come home she looks as she does every day."

The father said, "It is a very strange thing. I knew something was wrong, because I couldn't catch any animals."

The next morning Da-ne-da-do went out at the usual time as if he were going on the circle. When he was out of sight of the house, he turned back another way and stood in the forest opposite the door of his home. He saw the pail thrown after the boy. He heard his wife say, "Go, get some water. I want to wash your sister. You stay outside a while."

After she had said this, it was not long before she came out dressed in her best skins and beads. She looked at the path where her husband usually went out and at the path where he started toward the south. He watched her go into a swamp not far from the house. He could go home now for the bow and arrow which he had never used. He thought he would need them this time.

After getting his bow, he entered the swamp where his wife had gone, but he kept out of her sight. He followed her a long way from home until she came to a hill rising out of the swamp. A large dead tree stood there near another tree and leaned against it. The woman had a stick ready. She struck the dead tree, making a pleasant sound. She listened. Then she struck the tree again with her stick. All at once Da-ne-da-do heard something over his head in the air. He looked up. There was a flock of ducks. He saw that the ducks were bringing to the ground a man they were carrying in a robe. As soon as the man reached the ground, Da-ne-da-do's wife and this man talked and laughed. She asked him to sit down on a log with her. They talked. Da-ne-da-do crept as near as possible to listen. He couldn't hear all that they said, but he heard the man say, "We will put the robe on the ground and sit there."

The man spread the robe on the ground. He started to sit down. Then Da-ne-da-do drew an arrow and shot the man. The arrow went through the man's stomach. He threw himself upon the robe. He called the ducks. They came and carried him up into the air.

Da-ne-da-do's wife said to him, "What are you doing here?" They began to fight. She struck him down. She thought she had killed him, and she went back to her children. She said to them, "I have killed your father. He accused me of being with another man. I am going to my mother's home. I am going to destroy your home. You must care for yourselves. Your father abused me."

She took all of her things. She burned the house. She waited until it was all in ashes. Then she picked up some ashes and threw them into the air. She said, "It is going to snow until the snow reaches the treetops."

The mother went toward the east. When the fire was out, the children shivered. It began to snow.

Da-ne-da-do was not dead. As soon as he could, he went home. The boy said, "Mother set the house afire."

But the father said to him, "You need not worry about a home. You shall have a good one. You shall have a good black dog for a guide." Then he called, "Whu-de-gue-yue!" He called three times.

The snow piled up on the ground. A big dog came out of a hole in the ground. As he came out, the boy pushed his sister into the hole. Then he went in himself. They found that they were in a good house. Their father joined them. He said, "I am going to follow my wife. You will never be hungry. There is a kettle. All kinds of food are in it for you — hominy, deer meat, and bear meat. The food will always be cooking. Here is a pail of water that will never go dry. Do not go outside until the dog wants to go. The dog will be your guide."

Da-ne-da-do said to his son, "Where the dog wants to go, follow him. Always carry your sister on your back or lead her by the hand. Never leave her alone." Then Da-ne-da-do left to find his wife.

The children lived there happily. All their wants were supplied. It was a long time afterward when all at once the dog wanted to go outside. He smelled around the door. When the children opened the door, they found that spring had arrived. It was pleasant. Flowers were blooming and the birds sang joyously. The dog walked in a big circle and came back home. The brother and sister followed him. When they came back to the house, they helped themselves to the food. They slept well the night after their walk.

The next morning the children went out to pick flowers. When the boy grew tired of carrying his sister, he led her by the hand. On the third day they went farther. They came to a pond. A little duck was on the pond. The little girl wanted the duck. Her brother said, "No, you can't have it."

The girl cried, "I want the duck. I like the duck! Get it for me!"

At last the boy left his sister. He jumped into the deep water. When he was near the middle of the pond and very near to the duck, he heard his sister cry. He turned and saw a big bear pick his sister up and carry her off. The dog barked and growled and followed the bear. The boy got out of the pond as soon as he could, but by the time he reached the shore he was all alone. He began to cry.

After he had gone home, he thought, "I will follow the bear and save my sister." He started out quickly, forgetting his bow and arrows. He went a long way. He grew very tired. When night came, he lay down in the shelter of a fallen tree. This he did many nights. Every morning when the sun arose, the boy listened. Sometimes he thought he could hear the dog barking in the east. All he had to eat was berries. He wished he could die and end his misery. At last he came to a river. The river had a high bank of steep rock. The boy thought, "I can easily kill myself here."

He looked down to the river. He said to himself, "I will be dead before I strike the bottom."

So he stepped back. Then he ran and jumped off the rock. He seemed to fall for a long time. He kept thinking, "I wish I would die now. I am going to die now." When he struck the river he thought, "I am dead now for sure."

A big fish was waiting there. It swallowed him. He thought that of course he was dead. He had been a long time in the fish when suddenly he heard a voice.

Two sisters had set a trap to catch fish. The trap was a fish basket which they hung over the edge of the falls. As the fish came down the river, it fell into the basket. One woman said, "How lucky we are! Here is a big fish."

Both women seemed very much surprised. The boy listened. He heard one woman say, "We must dress the fish here. We can't carry it because it is too heavy. We will cut the head off."

It was still too heavy. The other woman said, "We will cut off the tail."

They cut off the tail. Then they began to roll the fish to the dry ground. When they got it to the dry ground, they cut the belly open. They took the innards out. The stomach was moving. It seemed very strange to them. The younger woman said, "Let us open it."

Carefully cutting the stomach open, they found the boy inside and were amazed. They were pleased with him, though, because he was a good-looking boy. Forgetting the fish, they took him home and fed him. Then they said, "We will keep this boy as a son. He is well formed and has been well brought up."

After they had decided this, they went and brought the fish home. The women asked the boy how he had gotten there and where he came from. He couldn't make them understand. Day after day they asked the boy, "Who are your relatives?" but he would not tell.

The two sisters gave him a bow and arrow. They said, "Go out and kill some birds in the north, south, and west. You must not go toward the east. If you do, you will have trouble, and we, too, will have trouble!"

One day he returned with a good many squirrels and birds. The women were surprised and pleased at his success with the bow and arrow.

The next morning they said to him, "You must not go toward the east. There is a big trench which bounds our land on the east. You must not go beyond it to the other land." The boy started as usual, but when he was out of their sight, he went east. He found the trench. He thought, "I can jump over it. I know I can."

He went back a way, ran, leaped, and reached the other side. He went on toward the east until he saw an open place in the woods. A log house was there, but no other buildings. The boy went to the house and looked through a chink between the logs. He saw an old man in the middle of the room. The old man was mending a fishing net and singing over and over, "My fishing net is broken and torn to pieces. I am mending it."

The man had great warts on his face. His eyes were sore and he was almost blind. The boy opened the door and said, "Hello, Uncle!"

The old man was so startled that he tore his net in two. He reached for his wooden mallet and tried to hit the boy. The boy shouted, "I am only a little boy. Don't kill me. Look at me."

The old man reached for an oyster shell. He scraped his eyes so that he could see. He raised his eyelids with his fingers and held his eyes open while he talked. He said, "You are a good-looking boy. Where did you come from?"

The boy answered, "My father is the man whose house is built of hemlock boughs."

The man said, "That is enough, that is enough. I know all about it. The bear took your sister while you were in the water after the duck. The bear passed near here with the girl. They were going east. Your mother met a man in the swamp. The man was brought there on a robe carried by ducks. Your father shot the man. Then your father gave you a good home and went to find his wife. I always know everyone who is passing by. You must be a witch boy, for I didn't notice until you were in the house."

The boy said, "I am from the home of the two sisters."

"That is enough, that is enough. Tell me the rest tomorrow," said the old man.

So the boy left the log house and went home another way as if he had not gone east. The next day he left home early. The sisters said, "You must not go east."

When he was out of sight, he went east. This time he went directly to his uncle's house. He did not know that it was the home of a man-eater. The boy looked through the chink in the wall. He saw the old man mending his net and singing, "My fish net is broken and torn into pieces. I am mending it. My fish net is torn and broken to pieces. I am mending it." The boy opened the door and said, "Hello, Uncle."

The old man was startled again. He tore the net. The boy told who he was. The man-eater put a bandage on his eyes to hold them open. Then they went on talking. The old man said, "There is a way to free your father and sister and dog. Your mother is to be married in a few days to another man. Then she will kill your father and sister and the dog. She wishes to end the family. I will give you a little advice, but keep it to yourself. The two sisters who have adopted you are very powerful sisters. No one ever stays there. All who have come have had trouble at once. The sisters have killed every one of them. But I know that they love you and they will do anything for you. Tonight you play sick, groan, get sicker and sicker during the night. They will give you a cloak made of the skins of human beings. They will give you a tobacco pouch and pipe. The pipe will go to the fire and come back lit. A loon is on the pipe stem. A sinew holds its beak. Remove the sinew and the loon talks. No one has ever seen these things or even heard of them. The sisters will try to comfort you because you are sick. They will give you all of these treasures. If all comes out right, come back tomorrow and let me know. Now run back to your mothers."

The boy went home. He had no game. He said, "I am so tired. I am so tired." He began to groan and say, "My head is sick. My body is sick."

The sisters tried to comfort him and make him feel better, but he grew worse. All night he lay there groaning. Toward morning the sisters brought him the cloak made of the skins of human beings. The boy grew a little better, but he was not well yet. They brought him the pipe and tobacco pouch. The tobacco pouch was made of marten skin. The boy felt better. The sisters said, "That is just what he needs."

Soon the boy was well. They said to him, "Whenever you put on the cloak, the skins will come to life. One man will be on one side of you and another man on the other side of you. Each of them will have a club. They will protect you always. You will never be harmed. Fasten the tobacco pouch and pipe to your belt. When you fill your pipe, the marten will go to the fire, get a coal, and light the pipe. If you want a little fun, unfasten the bill of the loon. The loon will cry. People will come out of the woods. Your cloak will kill them."

At daylight the boy wished to smoke. He filled the pipe. The marten of the tobacco pouch went to the fire and lit the pipe. The marten brought the pipe back to the boy. The boy smoked. Every time he whiffed the pipe, wampum came out of his mouth with the smoke. Soon wampum was all over the room. It lay all around him. It was most valuable. The sisters were pleased. They explained to him fully about the cloak and about the loon on the pipe stem. The boy said, "I will have some fun."

He went outdoors near the house. He took the sinew off the loon's bill. The loon cried. Men came in great numbers from the woods. The boy ran toward them. The cloak began to kill people. The sisters were happy because the pouch and pipe and cloak worked so well.

That morning the boy told his adopted mothers where he

came from. He said, "I suppose you have heard of my father, Da-ne-da-do." They answered, "Yes, we have."

He said, "When my sister was carried away by the bear, I started out to find her. But I grew tired and wished I were dead. When I came to the river with the steep rocky bank I thought, 'This is a good place to kill myself.' I jumped into the river and a fish swallowed me. You found me in the fish. That is how I came here."

They said, "We know from your story that you are going to get along well in life. You are going to succeed."

He said, "For the last two days I have been to see my uncle. I have had good visits with him. I am going again this morning. He told me to play sick. He said, 'You groan and get sicker and sicker. The sisters will do anything for you to make you better. They will give you the cloak made of the skins of human beings and the pipe and tobacco pouch which will light the pipe for you.' I am going to show him these things this morning. He will tell me how to save my father, my sister, and my dog."

The sisters did not forbid him to go. They were pleased because his father was the man whose house was built of hemlock boughs.

The boy headed for the house of his uncle. When he arrived, the old man was looking for him.

The old man said, "I heard the loon and knew that you were coming. Forbid the cloak to touch me or it will kill me."

The old man looked at the tobacco pouch made of marten skin. He looked at the pipe and at the loon on the pipe stem. He said to the boy, "I will tell you how to go to where your mother is living. Your father is sitting near the fireplace coughing. A stick is in his side to make him cough. The stick makes him full of misery. Your sister is hung over the fireplace. Every once in a while your mother stirs the fire. The fire makes the girl cry. The tears she sheds are wampum. They fall into the ashes. The mother saves the wampum.

"The dog is under the bed. He is dying. Every day they poke him with a burning stick. The man who had the duck robe is lodged in a hole in the roof over the fireplace. The arrow which went through him has come to the ground. It has grown up through the man into a tree. The man is still alive. Your grandmother, who can take the form of a bear, is there. She carried your sister away. Day after tomorrow your mother is going to marry the man who spits the most wampum.

"You'd better start soon. Go east. You will see a man in the path ahead of you. You call to him, 'Get out of my way. I am in a hurry.' If he gets out of the way he will not be harmed. If he does not get out of the way, the cloak will kill him. Farther on your way you will see two men in the path in front of you. You call out, 'Get out of my way. I am in a hurry.' If they get out of the way, they are unharmed. If they do not get out of the way, the cloak will kill them. All day you will see groups of men who are going to the contest to spit wampum. There will be as many as twenty men in some groups. Every time you see any men, call to them. If they get out of the way, all right. If they do not get out of the way, the cloak will kill them all. You will see many men before you get there.

"Just before you reach the house, go into the woods. Find a fallen tree that is hollow. Creep into one end of it. Leave your cloak in it. Creep out of the other end of it. Keep your tobacco pouch in your belt. Your mother has an open place cleared for the contest. She will sit on a rise of ground where she can see the men who come to spit wampum. Other men will be there to count the wampum. Your turn will come. You will spit the most wampum. The men who count the wampum will say, 'He is the man. Let him take the woman.' Most of the people will go home. Others will stand around in groups. You will say to them, 'Let us go to bed.' They will go to bed. Say to the house, 'Turn to marble and burn slowly.' Then you go into the house. You will find everyone asleep as if dead. After a while you will feel the house growing very warm.

"Find the dog tied under the bed and untie him. Go to your father and pull out the stick. Free your sister. By the time you get them out of the house, the fire will have burned the house and the people sleeping in it."

The old man was finished and shut his eyes. The boy set out toward the east. In a short time he saw a man in the path in front of him. The boy called, "Get out of my way. I am in a hurry."

The man looked around. He saw that it was only a boy who

was calling to him. He did not get out of the path. The cloak killed the man. A little farther on the boy saw two men in his path. He called out, "Get out of my way. I am in a hurry." The men did not get out of the way. The cloak killed them. The cloak killed all the men whom the boy overtook.

Before he reached the house the boy found a fallen tree that was hollow. He crept into it. Leaving the cloak inside of it, he crawled out the other end. He saw that there was a large number of people about his mother's house, including boys of his own age. In the afternoon he went to the door of the house. When the dog saw him, it yelped. His old grandmother poked the dog with a blazing stick. After a while the boy again went to the door. When the dog saw him, it yelped. This time, too, the old woman jabbed the dog with a blazing stick.

Evening came at last. Everyone stood around the open place where the men were going to spit wampum. A man with an oxtail tied on his head announced the contest. One by one the warriors came forward to see who could spit the most wampum. The first man spit two wampum. The wampum were carried away. The number of wampum kept growing larger. After the men had spit out all the wampum they could hold in their mouths, the man with the oxtail tied on his head asked the boys to try to spit wampum.

At last the son of Da-ne-da-do tried. He filled his pipe from his pouch. He set the pouch on the ground. The marten took the pipe and carried it to the fire. The marten brought the pipe back lit. The boy began to smoke. After one whiff there was a pile of wampum on one side of him. He took another whiff and there was a pile of wampum on the other side of him. He could not smoke more, for the judges cried, "That is the man. That is the man. There is no use staying. We have the right man."

The boy said, "I do not want the woman. I do not want to marry."

The judges tried to make him marry the woman. He said, "I will not."

Most of the people went home. Others stood around in groups. The boy said to them, "Let us go to bed."

They went to bed. He said to the house, "Turn to stone. Be very hot. Burn slowly."

He went into the house. He found the dog under the bed and untied him. The house was already growing warm. He ran to his father and pulled the stick out of his father's side. Then he cut the rope that held his sister over the fire. By this time the house was very hot. He led his dog and father and sister outdoors. By magic he made them well and strong again. Now the people in the house awoke. They cried, "Let us out. We are burning up."

The house was all marble now. They could not escape. It grew hotter and hotter. In a short time they were dead. Their bodies were burned up. The boy went back to the log and got his cloak.

Then the boy, his father, sister, and dog started toward the man-eater's home. Along the way, the boy told his father and sister all that had happened to him. When he had finished the story, he explained that his uncle wanted to see them.

It was a day's journey to his uncle's. The boy ran on ahead. When he reached his uncle's house, the boy said, "Everything happened just as you said it would. The cloak killed everyone who did not get out of my way. I found many men and boys there ready to spit wampum. I spit more wampum than any of the others. I saved my father and sister and dog, and burned the house with my mother, my grandmother, and the man with an arrow through his stomach. At sundown my father and sister and dog will be here."

The man-eater said, "I am going to be a different man now. I am not going to eat the flesh of human beings any more. I am going to eat the flesh of wild beasts. Then I will have no more warts on my face. My eyes will not be sore. We will live peacefully together. I will remove the trench. You will be the head man now, and you will look after all of us." He cleaned his horrible looking face and magically cured himself.

The boy went back to the sisters and said, "My father, Da-ne-da-do, and my sister and my dog will be here at sundown."

The sisters quarreled. The older sister said, "I am going to marry Da-ne-da-do." The boy said, "Stop quarreling. You have said enough." They said, "What time did you say they would be here?" The boy said, "They will be here at sundown."

One of the women went outdoors and said to the sun, "Set faster." The sun went down faster. About this time the travelers arrived at the man-eater's home. The man-eater said, "Come, let us go to the home of the two sisters." At sundown they came to the house of the sisters. Supper was ready for them. The sisters said, "The man-eater is a different man. He is a good-looking man now." One of the women said, "I will marry Da-ne-da-do." The other woman said, "I will marry the man-eater." After they had eaten their supper, they went outdoors. The man-eater and the other sister sat together in another part of the yard. The boy and his sister and dog sat in the doorway. It was twilight. They were all happy. They said, "This is our home. We will live together here."

They are probably living there yet.

CHAPTER THREE

The Boy Hero Who Saved His Father and Redeemed His Friends

The hero of our story is not Da-ne-da-do, but his son who is never even named. He is a boy, or the boy, the archetypal child in all of us, whose incredible courage and magical power can save us from any disaster. Two children were reported to be the founders of the Seneca nation by one source that we quoted earlier. They killed the uroboric dragon that had plagued their people. We find child heroes in nearly every mythology. Romulus and Remus founded Rome. Both Hercules and Sampson first gave promise of their adult prowess as infants. At the age of ten, many children move from the unconsciousness of early childhood into a beginning self-consciousness.

I was ten when I realized that I had the potential to deal with the world, although it was several years before I actually began to make use of it. As a school teacher, I found that ten-year-old children were the easiest to teach. Children of this age have not yet been touched by the turmoil of puberty and adolescence, and unless they have been damaged by home or school they are eager to learn. The Greek god Eros was usually pictured as a child or youth and was also designated as the creator of the world in some Greek creation stories. In his startling archetypal paintings, Birkhauser portrays this youthful figure astride a great beast with creative power exuding from his hands and body. In order to make contact with and give expression to this fertile energy, we need to allow ourselves to become child enough to be loved as a child, to use a phrase of Henri Nouwen. Then we can be enlivened by the very loving creativity at the heart of being. How many artists have tried to portray the young Jesus confounding the wise ones in the Temple?

Going back to the actual beginning of our story, we find the primal man, Da-ne-da-do, going out into the forest to create a place for himself. He is going into Dante's "dark wood," not in confusion, but with a clear plan. He has no ax. Primitive people from the dawn of time have had axes, but this man uses fire creatively to fell the trees and then burn them into usable lengths. Where the earth was warmed and the ashes fertilized the ground, Da-ne-da-do planted corn, the staff of life in Native America, the very life-giving gift that sprang from the breasts of the mother of humankind. Corn was sacramental to most Native Americans. Corn pollen was used among the Navaho in their sacred sand paintings; it was perceived as the elixir of life. Eating hominy and cornbread was symbolically partaking of the earth spirit herself. As ordinary bread is seen as the body of Christ by many Quakers, so eating corn was sacramental of being in touch with the Earth Mother.

As I first began looking at these stories, I was struck by the way Da-ne-da-do was designated throughout the tale — the man who lived in a house built of hemlock boughs. A great forest of hemlock grew across north central North America, the area occupied by the Iroquois. These dark evergreens had great spreading branches like the redwood. A few layers of the branches could act as thatch and provide a comfortable dwelling. In addition, the same branches, properly arranged, made a comfortable bed. When I was a child, my father and I camped in the forest and he cut down hemlock boughs and made our beds with these fragrant branches. He had been raised in Seneca country and knew the Seneca lore. From childhood he had camped along the Allegany River and slept on beds made of hemlock boughs. My father also planted a row of hemlock trees trimmed into a ten-foot hedge in the yard of the first home he owned to separate us from our neighbors. These trees were sacramental to him.

The man who lived in the house built of hemlock boughs was also a magical hunter. He did not need to use any weapon to provide game. He simply walked through the woods in a circular path in the morning and then in the evening retraced his steps;

any animals that stepped on his track died and he simply carried them home.

Deep in the human psyche is the fear of treading upon another's footstep. Children play games based on this fear. In his book, *Allegany Oxbow*, Charles Congdon writes reminiscences of ninety years of living among the Senecas on the Allegany Reservation. He tells two tales of his friends who had fetishes used in hunting. One fetish was believed to draw the game closer, the other made the hunters invisible so they could come close to their quarry. Both friends were very successful hunters. Da-ne-da-do lived well, and because he had killed many bear and had many deerskins filled with bear oil, he was a very rich man.

At this point a woman comes into the picture. In good Seneca "woman's choice" style, she comes to him with the traditional cornmeal wedding cakes made in the traditional way. She simply and directly states, "I have come to marry you." The marriage service is short. Da-ne-da-do completed the contract by saying, "We will live together." Although the reader has already seen the misfortune that follows, neither man nor woman can live alone and be fruitful. Each of us has within us both masculine and feminine, and we need to be in touch with both sides of ourselves if we are to be fruitful, even if this seems to be a dangerous undertaking. First was born the boy hero and then his sister, again symbols of both male and female. With the chief characters in place, the plot thickens.

One day many years later, Da-ne-da-do went out on his usual hunting walk and found no game when he retraced his steps. This happened the following day with the same result. He knew now that something was very wrong. He knew now that he had an enemy, that his magical power was gone because he had been bewitched. When he came home he asked his child, his inner childlike and totally honest son, what his wife did when he left to hunt. He was told that his wife dressed in her best beads and went out. She returned home and changed to her ordinary clothes before the hunter returned home. Sometimes, often in middle age, our feminine or masculine side goes berserk and looks for greener pastures; this often causes us to lose our creative power.

Da-ne-da-do decided to find out for himself what was going on. When we lose our inner energy or meaning, our power, we need to find out what has gone wrong. The next morning he pretended to go out hunting as usual, and then he saw for himself the scene that his son had described. He then followed his wife and discovered that she had found another powerful, magical man.

She called him to come by striking a dead tree. How often have we struck a hollow tree hoping that something magical would happen, that a magic carpet might appear from the sky? How frequently this image of the magical flight appears in all myths, the idea of teleportation in one form or another. On this hill in the middle of a swamp, her call was answered; ducks carried a blanket or robe in their beaks, with a man upon it. Perhaps these were the same birds that cushioned the fall of the grandmother (the Great Mother) of the human race. The man and woman talked to one another and then the man invited Da-ne-da-do's wife to sit on the blanket with him, hardly an innocent gesture in those circumstances.

The problem was now clear. The harmony has been broken and this has defeated his magical hunting. Da-ne-da-do put an arrow to the string of his bow and shot the man through the stomach. The victim called for the ducks, who came and carried him away. Husband and wife quarreled and fought. His wife struck him down with such force that she thought he was dead. She left him lying there and returned home to display the destructive side of the feminine, which is portrayed by Medea among the Greeks, by Delilah among the Hebrews, and Grindel in Norse myth. She took her valuables and burned down the house made of hemlock boughs. Then she threw the ashes of their house into the air and snow began to fall; winter descended. This mother was cold as ice. She left the children shivering and hungry and walked to the east.

As we have seen, the father was not dead, but returned to take care of the children. Not only has she destroyed their home, but like the despondent or angry Mother Goddess, she brings winter, the time when life goes dormant. She is frigid in her feelings for her children who would have perished had their father not returned. How careful we need to be of the cold destructive, vindictive side of the feminine within us all, of that reality Jung calls the negative side of the animal in man. Both men and women have a Hitler within them or a Medea who killed her children to get even with her unfaithful husband.

When Da-ne-da-do returned in the falling snow, his frightened son told him what had happened. But his father reassured the children they had nothing to fear. He then called the magical words, "Whu-de-gue-yue" three times and out of the ground emerged a good black dog. The father told the children to follow the dog into the hole from which the dog had emerged and they found a wonderful home under the dormant earth where life was preparing for spring. They found a magical pail of water that never went dry and a kettle of venison and bear meat and hominy that never gave out.

We are reminded of the widows who were kind to Elijah and Elisha, whose containers of oil and grain remained filled during a time of famine, and of the heroes who have been left to die and are suckled by wolves or goats or saved by strangers. There is indeed a never-failing source of energy and sustenance within us if we know how to find it.

In most Western mythology, the dog, like most genuine symbols, contains many meanings, both positive and negative. Among the Senecas the dog has little of the negative qualities found in many myths. The dog is the faithful one, the guide who personifies courage. In the White Dog ceremony a white dog was sacrificed and burned so that its spirit could carry messages to the Great Spirit. The ceremony was sometimes performed at funerals so the dog's spirit could lead the soul of the deceased along the strawberry road to eternal life. Although the white dog is seldom, if ever, sacrificed today, Congdon tells of his old Seneca friends who were present at this ceremony during their youth.

The children were told to stay in their underground home until the dog wanted to go out and then they were to follow their supernatural guide wherever it led them. Most of us need a period of incubation and retreat before we go forth on the hero's way, and then we need to follow the best spiritual guidance that we can find.

Before the father left he told his son not only to follow the dog, but always to carry his sister or lead her by the hand.

The dog, the instinctual guide, knew when life had returned and it was time to go out. They opened the door. Spring had burst forth in all its glory, flowers blooming, birds singing. The children went out to enjoy the new life of spring and to pick the wild flowers that grew in such profusion in Seneca-land in spring. Hesiod described how Persephone was picking flowers in just this way when the God of the underworld came out of the ground and seized her and carried her off to Hades.

Then came the act of disobedience that threw the children out of Eden. The children came to a pond and the little girl saw a duck in it that she wanted. Her brother refused, but when the girl cried hysterically the boy forgot that he was *never* to leave her alone and he swam out to get the duck. He then heard his sister cry again and, looking back, saw a big bear pick up his sister and run off with her. The dog followed, barking.

The bear is as universal and ambiguous a symbol as the dog. The basic difference between a sign and a symbol is that the former has essentially one meaning while the symbol has all the depth and mystery of any reality, physical or spiritual. The bear is valuable food, but it also represents the negative Great Mother, the unconscious. Russia is represented in most cartoons as a bear; the ancients named two of the most important constellations after the bear. One of the ancient pastimes was bear baiting. In this instance we remember from our story that this was the form taken by the girl's wicked grandmother. In *One More Story*, a book written in 1991 by Seneca DuWayne "Duce" Bowen, we find the same transformation of human beings into animals and back again to human form. The dark side of the unconscious always seems to be lurking around, ready to make the most of our mistakes and disobedience. How careful we need to be on the heroic journey, whether it is inner or outer.

When we find how miserably we have failed in following our destiny, we are often thrown into despair and depression. The boy followed the sound of the barking dog, but the sounds became less and less audible. In his hurry the boy forgot his bow and arrow; he could kill no game. He became very tired and hungry. Jung reminds us that hurry is not of the devil, it is the devil. When we are in a hurry, we seldom prepare for our journey. The boy wanted to die; he had lost all hope. He came to the high bank of a river and in utter despair threw himself into the river.

Like Jonah and innumerable other heroes he did not die, but was swallowed by a huge fish. He entered into the dark night of the soul, so well portrayed by the boy hero in the film *The Neverending Story*. The fish is one of the most significant symbols in dreams and myths. It usually points to some creative aspect of the deep unconscious. The fish was also an early Christian symbol. In Greek the first letters of each word of one of the earliest Christian creeds, Jesus Christ Son of God is Savior, are ICHTUS. *Ichtus* is also the Greek word for fish. This symbol is found throughout the Catacombs in Rome and was intended to give hope to those in persecution. The fish was certainly a savior for the boy. The fish died that the boy might live.

The two sisters who caught the fish could not carry it home because of its weight. They dressed the fish on the spot and found the boy in the stomach of the fish. They were delighted to find such a fine looking boy. They asked him how he got there and about his family, but he would tell them nothing. Sometimes it is best to keep one's spiritual identity to one's self. He needed to prove himself before he told his background; part of his reticence could have been his guilt. In good Seneca fashion they adopted the boy as their son. They gave him a bow and arrow and were again impressed that he could bring home many kinds of small game.

They warned him, however, when he went out hunting, that he must never go east. He could go in any other direction, but never east. Any healthy ten-year-old so warned will immediately be drawn east. The sisters were trying to protect him, but he had been through a lot and decided he would explore the forbidden territory. This time his disobedience was creative; he had hero work to do. The east is the place of the rising sun, the place of rebirth. It is the region of danger and potential and light. Herman Hesse has written of his own journey in his book, *Journey to the East*. Many Christian churches are built facing east.

The boy came to a ditch in the east, jumped over it, and soon found a log cabin. He saw an old man in the room singing to himself as he mended his fishnet. The boy went to the door, opened it, and called out, "Hello, Uncle!" When the old man heard his voice he picked up a mallet to attack the boy, but the boy with real presence of mind said, "I am only a little boy. Don't kill me. Look at me." When the old man had cleaned off his eyes with an oyster shell, he saw a good-looking boy and asked where he came from. Our hero boy was confronting the destructive aspect of the masculine; the man he faced was a man-easter, a cannibal, a male witch. The boy already knew the negative Mother. When we have the courage to deal with all that exists in the depths of ourselves, we may be ready to go on the hero's journey.

When the boy revealed that his father was the man whose house was made of hemlock boughs, he needed to say no more. The old man described to him exactly what he had been through. This clairvoyant man knew the boy was no ordinary child for he said, "You must be a witch boy, for I didn't notice you until you were in the house." Then the boy told that he had come from the home of the two sisters. The man-eater told him to go back to them and to return to his log house the next day.

As the boy left the following morning, he was again told never to go east, but he headed directly to the log cabin anyway. The old man was again surprised when the boy entered. This time he put a bandage on his eyes to keep them open. Then this potentially dangerous, wise old man told him that his father and sister and dog were being tortured by his mother and grand-mother. The mother was about to marry again and wanted to get rid of her former family.

He also warned the boy that he was living with two powerful and dangerous women, but they had magic fetishes that he could use to save his family. The old man then described to the boy how to get these powerful objects. The boy followed his directions exactly. He went home to the two women and pretended to be very tired and sick. All night he lay groaning. First they brought him the cloak made of human skins and he appeared to be a little better, but was not entirely well. Then they brought him a pipe with a bird on the stem (a loon that could talk). With it they gave him a tobacco pouch made of the skin of a marten (a weasel-like animal). No stranger or more powerful gifts were ever given to a Greek, Hindu, or Chinese hero.

When the boy recovered from his feigned sickness, the sisters explained to him the power of their magic gifts. When he wore the cloak, the skins would come to life and protect him from any enemies, killing them with clubs. I remember several people telling me of times when they were in great danger. They survived because they had the sense of two figures on either side of them, protecting them. The skins gave spiritual protection. The pipe was sacred to most Native Americans. Tobacco was used ritually and ceremonially, but seldom just for pleasure. The smoke from the pipe ascended to heaven and brought the smoker into the presence of the spiritual world. Tobacco was also put into the sacred fire as a burnt offering to the spiritual beings. The loon is a fish-eating waterfowl with a mournful cry that sounds like the voice of one who is crazy. When the boy hero took the sinew from the loon's beak, it would cry and people would come toward him; if they were dangerous, the cloak would kill them.

When the boy wanted to smoke, the marten skin came to life and took his pipe to the fire, lit it, and brought the smoking pipe back to the owner. The weasel was a royal animal and is frequently found in nearly all mythologies, sometimes as an instrument of the Great Mother, a disguise of Hera herself. Weasels were kept by Romans instead of cats because they killed snakes. Kipling told a story of modern India in which one of these animals (a mongoose) killed a cobra and saved a family. The weasel can be seen as a thief or a protector, another powerful and ambiguous symbol.

As the boy smoked the pipe, his mouth filled with wampum which he could spit out on either side of him until there were great piles of it. Wampum consisted of tiny beads that were one of the most valued possessions of the Iroquois, almost an equivalent to our symbol of money. Wampum belts were made with thousands of these beads worked into intricate designs. This magical pipe had the quality of the Midas touch; it could produce limitless wealth just by smoking it, a Seneca version of Aladdin's magic lamp.

The time had now come for the hero's total honesty. He now

shared his whole story with the sisters, including his background and his visits to the man-eater. They were pleased with his honesty and told him that he would succeed in life. In saying this, they gave him their blessing — and a powerful one from people able to produce gifts of this kind. They knew that he could protect himself and now did not forbid him to go east.

Off he went on his dream quest. When he met the father-like "uncle" he was told of the terrible situation his family was facing and was given instructions on how to save them. The boy did what he was told. He needed to hurry. When people paid no attention to him and would not get out of his way, his cloak would kill them. He arrived quickly at his mother's house, leaving his cloak in a hollow log. He found his family being tortured. His sister's tears became wampum. This illustrates the Iroquois attitude toward children and the total evil of the mother.

She was about to marry the person of the greatest wealth, the one who could "spit" the most wampum. First the men and then the boys tried to spit wampum. No one was a match for our hero. He was the winner and told that he could marry the mother, but he avoided Oedipus' fate by saying that he didn't want to marry. Many people left and he then told those who remained that it was late and they should go to sleep.

As soon as everyone was asleep, our supernatural hero used his magic power. He spoke to the house: "Turn to stone. Be very hot. Burn slowly." He spoke with creative power and soon the house grew very warm. He released his father and sister and dog and quickly took them out of the house. Then using his shamanistic healing power, he healed them of the wounds they had received. The people in the house awakened and cried, "Let us out." The house was now solid marble and getting hotter and hotter. In a short time they were all dead.

The boy and his family started off toward the cabin of the witch-shaman-man-eater. The boy told his father and sister about his adventures. He ran ahead to tell his "uncle" the wonderful success he had through following the old man's wisdom.

In some ways the most remarkable part of the story is its ending. When the witch-man-eater realized all the good he had done, he, too, was transformed. He told the boy that he was going to give up eating human flesh. He resembles the Iroquois Hiawatha who made the same decision. Then he healed himself of his ugliness and sores. He then said he would remove the trench, proclaimed the boy head man now, and promised they would live peaceably together and with the others as well.

The boy then ran on to tell the two sisters all the good news. Hearing that Da-ne-da-do was coming, they both decided they wanted to marry him. The boy immediately and with authority stopped their quarrel, telling them that the others would be there by sunset. Impatiently, they went out and spoke in a different way than Joshua, in the Bible. They said to the sun, "Set faster."

Sundown came quickly. The whole party arrived. The man-eater was now a handsome man. One of the women married him, the other married the boy's father. Peace and harmony reigned. The evil that could not be redeemed had been destroyed; the evil that could be transformed had been redeemed. How important to know the difference between these two evils within us and around us.

These Native Americans, living far from any European, African, or Asian influence, produced a myth of transformation using the very symbols found in Semetic, Egyptian, Greek, Chinese, and other cultures. How different, however, is the ending and tone of this story from the tragic endings of most Greek and Germanic mythology. The quality of harmony that created the Iroquois confederation permeates this myth as it did their league of equal nations. We can learn much from them and this story that they told. Transformation and redemption are possible.

CHAPTER FOUR

The Life and Death of Gan-nos-gwah, The Human Flesh Eater

In the fall of the year, a man and his wife prepared to go into the woods to make camp for the winter. They had a little baby girl. They packed enough provisions to last for a two-day journey. After bidding good-bye to their friends, they started for the woods to hunt and gather enough food for the winter. In two days they reached their camp and made it homelike.

After everything had settled down, the man went out hunting. He was not successful. He couldn't kill large animals. He killed only small animals, like rabbits, raccoons, and woodchucks. The family lived on the meat of these small animals for several days. Yet he had no better success. He and his wife talked about returning home. He said, "I am having poor luck. I can't kill deer, elk, or bears." His wife said, "Let us try to stay a few days longer."

Two or three days later, his wife went to the spring to get water. She left her child in the house, asleep. After she had filled her pail with water, she turned toward the house. As she came near the house, she heard something singing. When she came nearer, she realized that it was the voice of a human being. She could distinctly understand the sound. It seemed as though a strange woman were rocking her child and singing. The song was, "By o baby, it must be good meat. By o baby, by o baby, it must be good meat to eat. By o baby."

The mother was afraid. It sounded as though her baby would be eaten. She ran to the house. She looked in. A strange woman was sitting by the fireplace. She was holding the sleeping girl on her lap. The woman looked up at the mother and smiled. The mother was very much frightened. The woman said, "My name is Gan-nos-gwah. It is natural for me to live on the flesh of human beings. But you need not be afraid of me. I will do no harm to any of you. I came here to stay with you for the winter. I will help you all I can. You must be willing to have me here and I will serve you well. I go from place to place. I wish to stay here this winter. I am willing to share all the hardships of the camp with you."

Then she went outdoors and picked up sticks for fuel. She gathered a big pile of wood so that the hunter would not have to do it when he came home. Gan-nos-gwah tried to help in the house, too.

When the husband came home at night, he saw the strange woman. She spoke first. She said, "You need not be afraid of me. I came to help you. I know you. I have seen you often in the woods. You are not successful in hunting, and I am sorry for you. I came here to stay this winter. I told your wife that I wish to stay."

After supper she said, "I will help you kill game. I will cleanse you so that you can kill deer and elk and bears."

She had a peculiar kind of dish and a white pebble. She put water in the dish, she washed the white stone, and she took the water and sprinkled the clothes of the hunter. She said, "We will go hunting tomorrow morning before breakfast." She cleansed his bow and arrow with the water in which the white stone had been washed.

In the morning Gan-nos-gwah was up before the others. She built the fire. When the hunter arose, she said to him, "You start on ahead. Soon you will see a deer. Kill it, but let it lie. Go on further. You will see another deer. Kill it, but do not touch it."

He set out and had gone only a little way when he saw a deer. He shot it, but he did not touch it. He went on farther. He saw another deer. He shot it and let it lie. He kept on until he had killed six deer. Then he headed home.

He was almost at home when he met Gan-nos-gwah. She was smiling. She said, "I am late. I ought to have started sooner. I was delayed by work in the house." She went on smiling. He went into the house. He found breakfast ready. After he had eaten breakfast, he heard something drop in the yard. It sounded as though it was heavy. He looked out. Gan-nos-gwah had brought home all six deer at one time.

Gan-nos-gwah wore a dress made of stone. It was a kind of cloak. The stone was streaked with flint. It was a sort of shale, like a seashell.

She was fond of the baby. She often held the little child in her lap. Suddenly one day she said, "You must change the clothes of this little girl. There are spots on her dress which are turning to stone." The mother changed the baby's clothes. Gan-nos-gwah said, "You must change the child's dress every two days, or the dress will turn to stone. Then misfortune will come to the child."

Nearly every morning the father went hunting. Gan-nos-gwah always told him what direction to take. He always obeyed. She said every time before he started out, "You must not touch the game or try to bring it home." She went out after him every day and brought home all the game. It made no difference how much he had killed. She always brought it all home at one time. Gan-nos-gwah dressed and skinned the game. She built a frame of stakes and put a bark covering on them. On this she dried the meat outdoors. Sometimes she dried the meat over the fireplace inside the house.

All winter Gan-nos-gwah stayed with the family. They had plenty of game to eat. Gan-nos-gwah tanned the deerskins and made clothing for the family. She worked hard. She never did the cooking, but she did all the other work.

Every little while she would pick up the child and begin singing, "By o baby, by o baby, it must be good meat to eat. By o baby." This song always frightened and worried the mother. When Gan-nos-gwah put the girl down, the child would play on the floor. Gan-nos-gwah would look at the baby as though she wanted to eat her. She was sorry that she always frightened the mother. She said, "It is natural for me to eat the flesh of human beings. I cannot help it."

As spring drew near the hunter and his wife began to talk about going back to the settlement. They said nothing about it, but Gan-nos-gwah knew their thoughts. All at once she said,

"Whenever you get ready to go back home, I will help you pack up your things. I am very thankful to you. You have been very kind to me, to let me stay. I am well pleased by this winter I have spent with you." Then they thanked her for her help.

One morning she said, "Just let me know what day you wish to start. I have something to say to you then. I am going to give you something so that you will be always successful when you go hunting." From her clothes, she took a small mold made of stone. A white flint was inside of it. She gave it to the hunter. She said, "When you go hunting, put the stone in water in a dish and wash the stone. Then sprinkle your clothes and bow and arrow with the water. Drink a little of the water, but do not drink much. Then the animals will not be able to notice you at all. You can get as close to them as you wish. Before you start out hunting, think what you want to find in the woods. It shall appear before you. This is your pay for keeping me during the winter."

The hunter was very thankful. Gan-nos-gwah said, "Don't tell anyone that I have given you anything. You and your wife keep it to yourselves."

Then the hunter and his wife said to Gan-nos-gwah, "We are going to start for the settlement day after tomorrow." Gan-nos-gwah began to pack up things for them. She had the skins ready to pack their belongings in, and she said to them, "When you start for home, don't trouble yourselves with these bundles. I will take care of them. The second morning after you leave here you will find all these things piled up in the path in front of you."

The hunter, his wife, and child set out. Gan-nos-gwah stood and watched the man and his wife as they began their journey. They kept looking back at her and watching her. They thought that she might be following them.

It was still early in the spring. The snow was nearly all off the ground. There were bare places. In one of these, the hunter built a bed of hemlock boughs for his wife and child to sleep upon. The second day, in the afternoon, they came to the road. This road led to the settlement. There they saw their goods piled up in front of them. They had given half of the meat to

Gan-nos-gwah. Their half was waiting in the road for them. They found that everything was safely there.

They hurried home. They hired men with ox teams to carry the meat and fur and skins. It took three yoke of oxen to bring everything. According to the custom, the hunter and his wife called the people together and had a great feast. They provided a big meal for their friends. Their friends congratulated the hunter on his success in hunting and on returning home safely.

The hunter was successful ever after. He obeyed the instructions of Gan-nos-gwah. Their home had plenty of meat and they live there yet. Every time he wished to go hunting he took the stone and washed it in a dish of water. He sprinkled the water on his clothes and on his bow and arrow. Then he would think of what game he wished to shoot. And he and his wife have never spoken to anyone about Gan-nos-gwah or her gift to them.

GAN-NOS-GWAH DESTROYED

There was a man whose name was Ges-gar-doh. He bragged that he could kill Gan-nos-gwah. He was very brave. He was afraid of nothing. He was sure that he could kill the human flesh eater, Gan-nos-gwah.

Gan-nos-gwah lived in the woods. She could understand people's thoughts without hearing them talk.

One day Ges-gar-doh was walking on the flats along the river bank. He had his ax made of flint on his shoulder. As he went along, all at once he saw Gan-nos-gwah standing right in front of him. He was surprised. She spoke first. She said, "I have often heard that you have said, 'I can kill Gan-nos-gwah.' I am not afraid of you. I would just like to see you kill me."

The brave man was frightened. He ran. She followed him, but she could not catch up with him. Her stone coat made her clumsy. They came to a river. Ges-gar-doh, hoping to throw her off his track, forded the river. When he reached the other side, he looked and saw she was wading across to him. So he went back under the water to the other side. When Gan-nos-gwah reached the bank and saw him on the opposite bank which she had just left, she said, "I am going to get you anyhow." She started through the water again.

Then Ges-gar-doh doubled back on his path through the woods. He went around and around in circles, until he came to a tree that leaned against another tree. He climbed up and hid himself among the branches. But he did not puzzle her. Gan-nos-gwah did not follow him in his circles. Instead she came straight toward the tree where he was hiding. But she didn't know exactly where he was. She stood still under the tree. She put her hand inside of her stone cloak and pulled out a human hand. She put this hand on a fallen tree lying at her feet. She said to the hand, "Show me where Ges-gar-doh is." The hand pointed straight up.

Gan-nos-gwah could not bend her neck to see where he was. She could not look up into the tree. While she stood there, Ges-gar-doh jumped down and snatched the human hand quickly. He stood a little way from Gan-nos-gwah with it because he knew she could not follow him now. Gan-nos-gwah moaned and begged for the hand. She knew she could do nothing to Ges-gar-doh without the hand. All at once she saw the ax where Ges-gar-doh had left it. She ran her hand against the edge of the ax. This made the ax very sharp. With it she cut a stone in two as easily as if the stone had been a pumpkin. Gan-nos-gwah said to herself, "Ges-gar-doh can easily chop me to pieces with that ax." Ges-gar-doh stood near listening and watching. Gan-nos-gwah went to him.

"I want that hand of mine," she said. "Give it to me or I will die." He answered, "You always have said that you are brave. Why are you moaning?"

He walked around in a circle until he came to the ax. He picked it up and looked at it. She cried and begged him to give her the hand. He said, "I won't give it to you. I made up my mind when I came across a being like you, I would kill it."

She answered, "I might as well give you instructions. You must be careful how you treat my hand. I realize that I am going to die in a moment. You must keep the hand yourself and take good care of it. It will make you successful in hunting and in everything else. Use red sticks from the swamp to bathe and freshen the hand. Scrape the bark off the red sticks and squeeze the juice out of it. Preserve the hand by washing it in this juice. If the hand gets dry, it will be of no use to you. I know there is no hope for me. I can't escape. I might as well give myself up."

Ges-gar-doh laughed, for he knew what he was going to do with her. He said, "Is that all you wish to say?" Gan-nos-gwah had nothing more to say. Ges-gar-doh took his ax and cut off the head of Gan-nos-gwah. Then he cut her in pieces and threw the pieces in all directions.

Ges-gar-doh was very prosperous ever after, because he took good care of the hand and didn't let it get dry.

CHAPTER FIVE

The Kindness and Violence of a Witch

Our story begins in the fall. A man and his wife and baby get ready to leave the village settlement of several hundred people surrounded by several square miles of cleared farmland. This had been Iroquois and Seneca practice for generations. Winter was a time to live in the forest where the wind did not blow as violently and the snow did not drift as it did in cleared settlements. It was the time for hunting large game and smoking the deer and bear meat for spring when the villagers returned so that the women could plant their seeds and tend their gardens. When these stories were recorded, however, it had been a hundred and forty years since the Senecas had lived this way, another evidence of the age and authenticity of these tales of Seneca practice and belief.

Many of the families had semi-permanent forest camps to which they returned year after year. The family in the story took along enough provisions for the two-day journey. In their winter camp, other provisions had been stored. As soon as they were settled in, the man went out to hunt, but he could only find small animals that just kept them alive, giving them no real security or provision for the future. The man became very discouraged. The Seneca man who could not bring down deer, elk, and bears was a failure, and so the unnamed man in our story became depressed and wanted to return to the village where others would share their food with them if their supplies ran out. Among the Iroquois no one went hungry so long as anyone had food. The man's wife suggested that they stay on a few more days.

A few days later the wife left her baby asleep in their house and went outside to fill her wooden pail with water. As she came back near her house she heard the terrifying words of a woman's song coming from her house. "By o baby, it must be good meat. By o baby, it must be good meat to eat. By o baby." The frightened mother ran to the house and looked in the door. A strange woman was rocking her baby.

The central character of the story reveals herself. She is a powerful witch cannibal; her name is Gan-nos-gwah, but she means no harm to this particular household. She merely needs a home for the winter. They have nothing to fear. She explains that it is natural for her to eat human flesh. Today we might say that it is her addiction, but she will restrain her appetite while there and will help them and share her power with them.

If we survey the vast range of human culture, we find that cannibalism crops up in many different cultures. When meat and game was very limited and human life was cheap, the practice was a matter of survival. In addition, eating the flesh of a powerful enemy was sacramental; the eater ate it and by so doing shared in the power of the defeated enemy. The word "cannibal" comes from the New Latin word *canabalis*, meaning a member of the Caribbean Indian people. This word derived from the Spanish word *cannibal*, which was taken over from a native word, *Caniba* or *Carib*. The practice was believed by the Spanish to be common among these people. In Figi there are well-founded stories of chiefs who roasted their enemies alive and even ate part of their roasted flesh in front of the victims. In Africa many of the Pygmies who knew of the practice of cannibalism believed that their white overlords were cannibals because of their cruelty and because they misunderstood the meaning of the missionary communion service which spoke of eating Christ's flesh and drinking his blood. The early Christians were accused by the pagans of sacrificing babies and eating their flesh and blood in their predawn secret services of Eucharist.

In his paper, "The Transformation Symbols of the Mass" in Volume 11 of his collected works, Jung writes in detail of the death and eating of a child in an African village, a rite prescribed by the shaman so that the tribe would be saved. Jung suggests that, in spite of our revulsion at such a practice, this sacrificial sacramental act lies at a deep level in the collective unconscious. He suggests that the Christian Eucharist is a profound spiritual expression of our need to share in the divine life to survive. The ritual sacrifices of the Aztecs, and the bloody, multiple murders and dismemberments that are committed in nearly all fragmented societies by psychotic people seem to come from a misunder-standing of this deep, archetypal level. The life of the Iroquois peace hero, Hiawatha, shows that these people were nearer their unconscious roots than many modern cultures. As we read early Greek myths we find again and again stories of children who were slain and fed to their fathers as an ultimate act of revenge and scorn. These stories of dangerous witch man-eaters are really demonstrating how wrong this cannibalism really was.

Returning to our story, Gan-nos-gwah told the husband that she would not only stay for the winter and help them with chores, she would also make him a great hunter. After supper she initiated him to a magical ritual. She brought out a white stone.

The white pebble has many meanings. It was used in the Greek and Latin world for voting. The white pebble indicated approval, the black one was a negative vote, and so our word, "blackball." In *Hamlet*, shards, flints, and pebbles are thrown on the grave of the deceased. White stones were sometimes used as love charms. Many of us get attached to a particular smooth stone. Precious stones have a compulsive attraction for some people.

Gan-nos-gwah put the pebble in a dish and washed it with water, then she sprinkled the hunter's clothes and his bow and arrow with the water. The water absorbed the power of the stone and conveyed it to the man.

Few symbols have more universal and diverse meaning than water. People of all cultures dream of water, of rain and the ocean, of rivers and lakes, of bathing and washing. In a real sense the water is the universal mother out of which life emerged and developed, and so water can refer to the deepest level of the primal unconscious. It also symbolizes cleaning. The first rite on coming to the healing shrines of Aescylapius was a ritual bath. The convert to Christianity is baptized with water. Holy Water is found at the entrance of many sacramentally oriented churches. Jewish law calls for ritual cleaning of dishes used for food. Moslems wash before they enter most mosques. Rivers of water flow from the city of paradise, described in the concluding book of the New Testament. In an arid country water is life itself and can symbolize the human soul. In this rite, the witch-shaman is cleansing and empowering the hunter with water that carries the power of the mysterious white pebble.

Gan-nos-gwah then gave further instructions: When the man killed a deer he must leave it lying where it fell. From that day on the man was able to provide a bountiful supply of large game. The first day he brought down six deer and left them lying in the forest. The same morning the witch went out and brought back all six in one load. She dressed, skinned, and dried the meat; she tanned the hides and made clothing for the family.

Gan-nos-gwah loved to pick up the child and sing her a strange lullaby, which always frightened the child's mother. "I love you so much I would like to eat you" is a common statement and may have deeper significance than we realize. Freud believed that violence and sexuality were closely related.

The witch had another peculiarity. Her dress was made of stone. After she had held the child for an hour, spots of stone appeared on the baby's clothing, stone streaked with flint, shale that was like seashells, just like Gan-nos-gwah's clothing. She warned the mother that the child's garments must be washed every other day or disaster could occur.

How seldom we realize the depth and variety of meanings that our words carry. We have already seen some of the less common meanings of pebble and water. As we reflect on the word stone, we find still another word of power. Idols hewed from stone representing gods are found in most ancient cultures. Many people who disobeyed the Greek gods were turned to stone as Lot's wife in the Bible was turned to a pillar of salt. Being as hard as stone can indicate strength and also lack of feeling, or stubbornness. Stone rubbing seems to be deeply instinctual and may represent the desire to make one's soul as smooth as one had made the stone. Whirling stones has been a common practice of rainmakers, probably symbolizing the fertile marriage of heaven and earth.

We could go on and on, as Ad de Vries does in his exhaustive *Dictionary of Symbols and Imagery*, but let us look at one more meaning he does not suggest. In the New Testament in I Peter 2:4 we read, "Come to him, the living stone, rejected by men, but approved, nonetheless, and precious in God's eyes." The stone here represents resurrected new life for those who value the resurrected one and a stumbling block of stone for those who do not understand this meaning. Even more mysterious is the white stone mentioned in Revelation 2:17. "To him who conquers I will give some of the hidden manna, and I will give him a white stone with a new name written on the stone which no one knows except him who receives it." Revised Standard Version[1].

Gan-nos-gwah knows telepathically when the young family intends to return to their village. She then gives the hunter the white pebble in a box or leather bag which is the probable meaning of the Seneca word translated "mold." She adds another suggestion to her ritual of the pebble and water. The hunter is to wash the white pebble, sprinkle the water on his weapons and his clothing, and then drink some of the water, in order to take its power into his inner being. Then the friendly, man-eating witch helps them pack and tells them to go to the village. Their possessions arrive at the settlement before they do, and the villagers help them put away the dried meat and clothes that they have accumulated during the winter. Food and clothing will be shared with others who need them.

Gan-nos-gwah then disappeared. She evidently had no plans of reforming as did the man-eating friend of Da-ne-da-do's son in the previous legend. She was evidently well known and a hero appeared on the scene to destroy her; his name was Gesgar-doh. He was very brave, frightened of nothing, and he bragged that he could kill the cannibal witch. Walking through the forest with his flint ax over his shoulder, he was suddenly confronted by Gan-nos-gwah who scornfully told him that she knew his intentions and that she had no fear of him. People with spiritual, magical power need to be careful of their pride or hubris, of their arrogance; this trait can destroy them. The ancient Greeks believed that the gods resented humans, particularly people with spiritual power, who boasted of their power.

In spite of his professed bravery, our hero was very frightened and fled. Gan-nos-gwah followed, but was hindered by her stone cloak. Ges-gar-doh tried every trick he knew to throw her off his track and finally climbed up into a tall tree. The witch's clairvoyant powers led her directly to tree, but evidently her stone clothes (representing her invulnerability) made it impossible for her to look up into the trees. She could not look up, a telling and significant flaw in her power. Therefore, she couldn't know exactly where her enemy was hiding. So she took out of her coat a preserved human hand, put it on the ground, and asked it to show her where her would-be destroyer was lurking. The hand pointed up.

The dried, human hand is a common fetish. The hand is another symbol with dozens of meanings. We still use it in signs to point out directions. The hand also separates human beings from most of the less-advanced animals. It enables us to make things, to hang on, to deal with and "hand-le" our lives. In dreams the hand is often a symbol of our capacity to manipulate (the word comes from the Latin word for hand) and deal with our problems. In Brazil the human hand with the thumb thrust up between the index and middle fingers is a good luck charm, known as the *figi*, and it is highly revered.

Ges-gar-doh jumped down from his ambush and snatched the hand from the ground. The witch began to moan and beg him to give her hand back. She even told her secret, "Give it to me or I will die." The hand gave her the power to contact spiritual powers and "handle" them. She picked up the ax and in touching the ax she sharpened it so that it could cut stone as if it were a pumpkin. Mythology is filled with magic weapons. However, for some reason not told, she cannot use the ax. She realizes that her end is near. Then the witch gives her attacker instructions on how to preserve and use the hand. It is almost as if she is in the service of the hand and that the hand is more important than she. The magic of perpetuating the power of the hand reminds one of an incantation. Let's read the instructions once more. Ges-gar-doh is to keep the hand for himself and it will give him every kind of success. "Use red sticks from the swamp (of all environments, the one most abundant in life) to bathe and freshen the hand. Scrape the bark off the red sticks and squeeze the juice out of it. Preserve the hand by washing it in this juice. If the hand gets dry, it will be of no use to you." The witch gave her destroyer the magical elixir that could keep safe his magical power.

Ges-gar-doh then took up his ax and cut off her head. Death had been the prescribed penalty for withcraft for centuries among the Iroquois. The hero was simply carrying out the law of his people in destroying one who used spiritual powers for destructive purposes. The hero went further and cut her in pieces and scattered them so that there would be no chance of her coming to life again. From then on Ges-gar-doh took good care of the magic hand and was able to handle his life with great success.

CHAPTER SIX

Ho-dar-da-se-do-gas

A boy had the habit, when he was through eating, of wiping his mouth with his hand and then wiping his hand on his feet. His name was Ho-dar-da-se-do-gas. When he smoked and had any tobacco left, he threw it into the fire and called aloud, "Qua-nos, Qua-nos!" Every time he finished smoking he called, "Qua-nos, you may have the rest of my tobacco." No one knew what Ho-dar-da-se-do-gas meant.

The young man grew up. One year he went hunting with a party of ten. They camped in the woods and were successful in hunting. One day, when they had been in the camp for quite a long time, Ho-dar-da-se-do-gas came back to the camp and said, "I have found a bear in a hollow tree." The next morning the men said, "We will go with you to this tree, and we will have some fun with this bear."

They went and stood together around the tree. The young man who had the habit of greasing his feet and of giving tobacco to Qua-nos, climbed the tree. He bent the tree. He set fire to a twig and dropped the twig into the hole in the tree. Then he went and leaned against another tree. An animal came out of the tree.

It was not a bear. It was a lizard almost as large as a bear. It had the name of Ci-a-nos. It was green with streaks about its mouth. It was lively and very quick in action. The men were astonished and afraid when the face peered out of the hole in the tree. When they saw it was Ci-a-nos, they ran away.

Ci-a-nos chased one of them. He overtook the man, killed

him, and brought him back to the tree. Then he went after another one. He overtook and killed him, too, and brought him back to the tree. So he ran down all the men, carrying each one back to the tree before he started for the next. He had to go a long way to get the ninth man.

Ho-dar-da-se-do-gas had climbed into a tree and was holding on by the limbs of the tree. He decided that he must run for his life. His habit of oiling his feet made him a faster runner. He had gone quite a distance when he heard Ci-a-nos coming after him. The young man thought that he must die. Suddenly an animal stood before him. It said, "Go under my body to the other side of me. You have always given me tobacco."

It was Qua-nos. Qua-nos was a strange animal. He had no hair, and his sweat was blood. He had big eyes, a big mouth, and big teeth. He was short-legged, but he had a large body. He attacked Ci-a-nos. Qua-nos and Ci-a-nos fought. At last Qua-nos killed Ci-a-nos. Then Ho-dar-da-se-do-gas took out his tobacco pouch and he and Qua-nos had a smoke together. After this Ho-dar-da-se-do-gas remembered every time he smoked, wherever he was, to spill some tobacco and say, "Qua-nos, you enjoy the rest of my smoking."

When they were finished smoking, Ho-dar-da-se-do-gas thanked Qua-nos for his help. Ho-dar-da-se-do-gas did not go back to the hunting camp. He said farewell to Qua-nos and started home. He told the people in his settlement what had happened. He said, "Ci-a-nos killed nine men who were with me, and Qua-nos killed Ci-a-nos and saved my life."

The friends of the dead men said, "We will go and see the dead Ci-a-nos, and bury our friends." They went to the place where Ci-a-nos was killed by Qua-nos. Qua-nos had disappeared. They went to the hollow tree where Ci-a-nos had carried the nine dead men. The friends took care of the dead bodies and buried them on the top of the ground. They set up poles in the ground. They put poles crossways on top and covered them with bark. They put the bodies on the bark high in the air. The men left the bodies there and then they had a council among themselves.

They said, "Ci-a-nos was a bewitched animal. We are going

to have part of its body, the teeth and claws and flesh, and make charms out of them."

One man said, "I am going to take its teeth so that I can be a hunter and any time I desire to kill an animal, it will come before me." He took the teeth of Ci-a-nos.

The second man said, "I will take a piece of its flesh so I can be charmed. I wish to have property, a home, and be wealthy." He took a piece of the flesh.

The third man said, "I am going to take the claws, so that I can get a woman. When I get a woman, I wish to have her follow after me." He took the claws.

The other men didn't take any of the animal. They were afraid.

The man who took the teeth was successful. Whenever he went hunting, he burned tobacco. He told the teeth what animals he wished to catch and the animals came. He was successful because of the teeth of Ci-a-nos.

The second man became very rich. It was easy for him to gain wealth. Everything he needed came to him.

The third foolish young man, at New Year's or Green Corn dances, burned tobacco and wished for the women to follow him. They hung about him and bothered him. He said to them, "Keep away!" They would not do it. He never married. He saw too much of women and quarreled with them.

The first man who was a hunter lives in the woods yet, and the animals still come to him.

The second man is still wealthy.

The women are still after the third man, and he is tired of them.

CHAPTER SEVEN

Mythical Dragons and Monsters

Although European etiquette would frown on Ho-dar-da-se-do-gas' table manners, many people throughout the world still eat with the fingers of the right hand, reserving the left hand for more menial service. I have observed this in Africa, Asia, and even in a Los Angeles Morrocan restaurant. From early childhood our hero wiped the grease from his mouth with his hand and then wiped his hands on his feet; this made him fleet of foot. He was also pious; whenever he smoked he threw any remaining tobacco into the fire and called out, "Qua-nos, Qua-nos!" And when he finished smoking he would again call, "Qua-nos, you may have the rest of my tobacco." We must remember that offering tobacco among most Native Americans was a way of relating to and pleasing the spiritual powers.

The boy grew up to become a young man and one year a group of ten went hunting together. Ho-dar-da-se-do-gas discovered an animal in a hollow tree. He thought it was a bear and shared his discovery with his companions who thought it would be exciting to have some fun with the bear. Our hero climbed a tree and set fire to a twig and dropped it down the hollow tree on the animal, but the animal that bounded out of the tree was no bear. It was a monstrous lizard as large as a bear. Its name was Ci-a-nos; it was green with streaks around its mouth. The hunters were terrified and ran away. One by one the agile and speedy monster caught each of Ho-dar-da-se-do-gas' companions, killed them, and dragged them back to his tree. Because our hero had oiled his feet, he was a very fast runner. He was able to keep ahead of Ci-a-nos for a time, but was tiring rapidly and his pursuer was coming closer. Then suddenly another monster stood in front of him who said to him, "Go under my body to the other side of me. You have always given me tobacco."

We are not told how this young man had learned of Qua-nos, but it was probably through a dream, for it was through dreams that the Iroquois believed they were given access to the world of spirit. They made masks of the creatures they saw in dreams and used them ceremonially. This monster was no more attractive than the other. It was hairless and its sweat was blood; it possessed a long, low body with short legs and great teeth. Qua-nos attacked the other monster. It was a furious battle, but Qua-nos finally killed Ci-a-nos.

It is important to keep in mind the basic idea of totemism: the spirits and animals that represented them were really indistinguishable. The animal was the spirit and the spirit was the animal. Jung points out in his article, "The Phenomenology of Spirit in Fairytales," that animals in fairytales usually represent spiritual powers and realities. The more bizarre and monstrous the creature, the more powerful the spirit it represented. Our tale presents us with two monsters as strange and powerful as any in Greek, Chinese, Hindu, or Persian mythology. Monster-dragons are found in nearly all mythologies. They are often related to the Great Mother Goddess. They sometimes stand for chaos that must be subdued. In the Persian creation myth when the primal monster was slain, the various parts of its body became the earth and the sky. The Hebrews often spoke of the sea monster, Leviathan. Dragons were guardians of the golden fleece and of the Golden Apples and other treasures (the dragon hoard).

In the form of a snake, the evil fallen angel, Satan, first appeared to Adam and Eve. September 29th is still celebrated as the day commemorating St. Michael's victory over the Satan who is often pictured as a dragon. In this story we find the same theme as the alchemists gave in their account of the struggle of the dragons by which the elements are separated. Young children often dream of strange monsters and draw pictures of them. Dragons can be evil, ambivalent, or creative.

In a zoo in Surabaya in Indonesia we saw two commodo monsters mating. These creatures are some fifteen feet long and are the closest remaining relative to dinosaurs. What in the depth of us calls forth the monster of Beowulf, Medusa, the Minotaur, the Sphinx, the many-headed dog who guards the entrance to Hades, the incredible monsters and dragons of China and Japan? There were no particularly strange creatures in northeastern North America, and yet here in a Seneca legend we find the same image. In China the dragon is a positive force and one of the signs in their astrology. In the film, previously mentioned, *The Neverending Story*, a beautiful furry, protective dragon saves the hero. Dozens of books could be written on the dragons and monstrous creatures found in the literature and mythology of the human race. These horrible creatures who are more than just animal totems may well represent nonphysical realities, principalities and powers of which nearly every religion of humankind speaks. The story is a warning not to play around with any potent spiritual power. If one does, only a creative, helpful, spiritual power can save one; one cannot save one's self. We must remember that in primal religious thinking the physical and spiritual reality of these creatures were not separated.

Once the battle was over and Ho-dar-da-se-do-gas regained his composure, he took out his pipe and tobacco pouch and he and Qua-nos smoked together. This was far more than two comrades smoking together on a summer evening. This was a religious rite, the hero's burnt offering to the powers that peopled the spiritual world. These spiritual realities could manifest themselves in the physical world at any time as well. Smoking the peacepipe, the sacred pipe, was a deeply religious gesture in which human beings and spirits shared together. Sharing his pipe and tobacco with Qua-nos was an act of communion, a sacrament.

We mentioned earlier the elaborate rituals used to bury the dead and help the Senecas deal with their grief and fear in an uncertain and dangerous world. The hero pauses and reflects on the value of his tobacco ritual offered to Qua-nos and vows to continue it. He then returns to his village to tell the story of the death of nine of their warriors and of Ci-a-nos as well. To the Seneca failure to take care of the bodies of their dead companions not only showed lack of human caring, it was sacrilegious. The dead who were not properly cared for might return and haunt those who did not dispose properly of their dead bodies.

The friends then exposed the bodies to the air on top of the ground (not under it as had been the custom for nearly a hundred years before these stories were told). They built a high platform of wood, covered the top with bark, and laid the bodies upon it — another indication of the age of these stories.

Among the ancient tribes in Georgia, huge mounds were built around burial sites. The platforms on which the bodies were laid were similar to those decribed in this story. In the Andes mountains east of Arica, Chile, eight-thousand-year-old mummies have been discovered. Among the Navaho, the dying person was often put outside the hogan (the Navaho home) because it could not be used again if a person died in it. Among the Hebrews, any priest or levite who touched a dead body could no longer serve in the temple. This puts the story of the Good Samaritan in a different light. Something deep within the psyche knows dead bodies are sacramental of the spirit that is gone and need to be treated respectfully. Graves of Neanderthal people, sixty thousand years old, show evidence of funeral rites.

Once these funeral rites were concluded, three men held counsel with one another. A remarkable opportunity lay before them. Since Ci-a-nos had been a magical animal (one that was both a powerful creature and potent spirit) the parts of its body would continue to be imbued with power. Many Christians keep relics of the saints for the same reason. The body of the one close to the Divine is believed to retain some of the divine power that was expressed in that person. The three friends decided to keep the monster's teeth, claws, and a piece of its flesh so they could make charms or fetishes of them.

The first man chose the teeth. The Greek hero Cadmus slew a horrible dragon and was told by Athene to take the dragon's teeth and sow them in the ground. From these teeth sprang wild armed giants that Cadmus couldn't deal with. At the goddess' suggestion, he threw a *stone* among them and they fell upon each other until only five remained. These came with Cadmus to found the ancient city of Thebes in central Greece. In dreams teeth often refer to one's ability to bite into life and to hang on. Loss of teeth often signifies lack of this power. The teeth of Ci-a-nos gave their owner the power to be a great and happy Seneca hunter. The animals still come to him. In a later story we shall see the power of a beaver's tooth.

The second man took a piece of the flesh. He believed that this would bring him wealth, property, and a home. How the Hebrews hated to leave the fleshpots of Egypt! The witches' brew in many cultures is made of the flesh of toads, bats, and other repulsive creatures. The flesh represents the physical and material side of human nature and also earthly riches. Ambiguous as all real symbols, it can also refer to the transitory nature of life or to sexuality. To St. Paul it was the part of our nature that warred against the spirit. Flesh also refers to earthly wealth. Polynesian kings often became huge in weight and size as a symbol of their wealth and power. The man with Ci-a-nos's flesh indeed became wealthy. Whether or not he was happy we are not told.

The third man was not as wise as the others. He took the claws. We can do no better than quote his words, "I am going to take the claws, so that I can get a woman. When I get a woman, I wish to have her follow after me." The claw often signifies ferocity, the law of the jungle and the talon, *lex talonis*. Shakespeare writes, "claw no man in his humour;" do not flatter another. Claws were also put on criminals as a symbol of their being in the clutches of the law. The eagle with its fierce claws is a totem of the United States of America and symbolizes its power. But the claw can also refer to degenerate sexuality, the desire to clutch and possess and use, what Freud sees as implicit in sexuality. This last meaning is the one referred to in this story. The foolish young man burned tobacco (prayed) at two of the major Seneca festivals for women to follow him. From then on the women hung around him, pursued him. He could no longer call his life his own. He never married. He saw too much of them and quarreled with them. This part of the story is a warning to the men who are emerging from a matrilineal society that having too many women interested in them, too much promiscuity, seldom brings happiness.

The hero of the story, Ho-dar-da-se-do-gas, undoubtedly being a good Seneca, took the teeth.

CHAPTER EIGHT

The Bear Trail

A boy lived alone with his uncle. Each morning, before his uncle left the boy, he would say, "You may go north and south and west of the house. You must not go east."

The boy hunted in the north and south and west, just as his uncle said. At last the game became scarce. He said to his uncle, "The game is scarce in the north and south and west. Can't I go east?"

The uncle said, "If you disobey me and go east, you will have trouble."

One day the boy saw a large deer. He started to follow it. Before he realized it he was east of his house. He looked about him. He listened. The woods were full of the sounds of game. But it was late in the day so the boy went home.

The next day the temptation was too great for him. He hunted in the north. Soon he began to go east. He saw an elk. He shot it and brought it home.

The next morning he started early and went directly east. Soon he came to a bear's trail. The steps were full of bear's oil. He followed it a way, but it began to grow late. He hurried home. He made up his mind to follow the bear's trail the next day.

His uncle went away in the morning. Then the boy set out. He found the bear's trail. It led towards the east. He followed it, going over mountains and through valleys. He crossed streams and made his way through thick forests. Days and days he traveled. He grew very tired. He knew he was far from home. At last he grew discouraged. Wandering on a little farther, he came to a mountaintop and sat down to rest. He saw in the valley, away in the distance, a little house. He hurried towards it. He thought he would find where the bear's trail led. At last he reached the house. The door was open. The trail passed close to the house. In the house were an old woman and her five daughters. They were grinding corn.

He said, "Will you tell me where this trail ends?"

One of the daughters came to the door. She said, "Do you see yonder mountain? Go to the foot of it, and go up this side of it and down the other side. Go through the valley to the next mountain. Go over that, through the next valley and over the mountain next to that, and in the valley you will find a house. Ask the people there where this trail leads."

The boy started on. He climbed the first mountain, descended, and crossed the valley. He went over the next mountain and through the valley. He went up the mountain next to that valley. He reached the top. He sat down to rest and looked down into the valley toward the east. He could see far away in the distance a little log house. He walked as fast as he could until he came to that house. The door was open. A woman and her five daughters were there. He went to the door.

He asked, "Can you tell me where this trail ends?"

A young woman came to the door. She pointed towards the east. She said, "Folow this trail over that mountain, through the next valley, and up the side of the next mountain. There it ends."

The boy went on. He went over the first mountain and through the next valley. He started up the next mountainside. He could see a little house on the mountaintop. He ran towards it. He was very tired of his journey and was anxious to see where the trail ended. As he came near the house, an old man tottered out of the house. The old man saw the boy. In a cry of welcome, the old man said, "My son, my son, you have come back to me!" The boy did not understand what the old man meant. The old man led the boy into the house.

He said to the boy, "You are my son. Your uncle is not your true uncle. He is my enemy. He robbed me and took you away. I thought that I would never see you again, my boy. We must not talk now. We must get ready for your uncle, for he will come after you. He takes the form of a bear and this is his trail. You go outdoors and get some pine wood. Bring it in the house. We will cut it into splinters."

The boy went outdoors. He brought into the house an armful of pine stocks. The boy and his father cut them in long thin splinters. Soon they heard the roaring and growling of an angry bear. The father said, "Here comes my enemy. Let this house grow very small! Let the door be so small that the bear can get only his paw in the door. My son, sit by the fireplace and keep the fire burning. The bear will put his paw in the door. You light a pine splinter and set the bear's paw on fire. Keep on lighting the splinters and sticking them on the bear's paw until the paw is all ablaze."

The bear came nearer and nearer. He growled and growled. The house grew smaller and smaller. The bear came near the house. He growled, "I will get you anyway, nephew." He put his paw in the doorway. The boy had the pine splinters ready. He set fire to the bear's paw. The bear howled with pain. The bear suffered terribly. He did not know what to do. Seeing a well nearby, he thought, "I will jump in the water and put this fire out." He ran to the well and jumped in. The well was a well of oil instead of water, and the bear's paw set the oil on fire and the bear was burned up. The boy's wicked uncle, his father's enemy, was dead.

The father said, "Let this house grow large again."

The house grew large. The boy and his father live there happily yet.

TWO CAPTIVES

One time a whole settlement was beaten by another tribe that was on the warpath. They spoke a different tongue, and they killed many of the people of the settlement. Several young men, however, were taken captive.

The warriors took the young men to their settlement, in the east. When they arrived with their captives, a great feast was prepared. The people built a big fire. They let it burn down until only ashes were left. The captive young men were told to walk through the fire. They walked back and forth until their feet were blistered. Then the blisters were pierced and kernels of corn were placed in the blisters. Two of the men with blistered feet were chosen to run a race to a certain mark.

They talked and planned together in their own tongue. One man said, "We will jump over the crowd when we are close to the mark. We will knock some people over and escape if we can't jump over." The men started to run. People crowded up on both sides. The young captives were nearly to the mark. Suddenly they jumped into the air. They cleared the heads of the people and were away before the people knew what had happened. The warriors followed the brave young men until dark, but they could not catch up with them.

During the night the young men ran on. In the morning they jumped into the river. They hid under projecting banks during the day. During the night they swam in the river. In this way they neared their home. As they went through the water, they imitated the sound of ducks. They did this so that people would think the moving of the water was caused by ducks. In one place, people were camping on the shore eating deer meat. They heard the "quack, quack" in the water. To scare the ducks away, a man threw a bone at them. The bone hit one of the young men in his mouth. It knocked his teeth out.

The men at last reached their own tribe. Their feet healed, but one man was without teeth for the rest of his life.

CHAPTER NINE

Captivity and Release

A boy lived with his uncle. As we noted before, this was the natural family situation in a matrilineal society that had existed without a break for a hundred thousand years until a few thousand years ago. When a woman had more than one partner, the question of paternity was ambiguous. The clan, the mother, and her brother usually raised the child and the uncle became the significant male figure in the child's life. This boy, or more probably a young man, was a fine hunter. He was encouraged by his uncle to go out in search of game so long as he did not go east. We find the same prohibition here that we found in our first myth. Perhaps in this story going east signifies independence, manhood, freedom as well as consciousness, leaving bondage, and taking charge of one's own life. The youth is warned of serious trouble if he disobeys and goes east. Consciousness is dangerous and those who seek it can seldom turn back without disaster. East was also the direction the Iroquois traveled to find the lush forests of Central New York State. If we cannot go east, half the world is hidden from us.

One day when the youth was hunting, he saw a large deer and followed it east. He looked about him. He listened. The east was full of life and game, but since it was late he returned home. The next day he started north, but soon found his feet carrying him east. He came upon an elk, shot it, and brought it home. His curiosity was now aroused and the next morning he went directly east, into the forbidden territory. He came upon a bear's trail; the tracks were full of oil – wealth to the Iroquois.

It became late and so he returned home again, but made up his mind to follow the tracks he had found.

As soon as his uncle left, our nameless hero set out. He found the bear's trail and followed it through thick forests, over mountains, and down into valleys. As children we sang a song (and children's songs often have more meaning than we realize): "The bear went over the mountain, the bear went over the mountain, to see what it could see." The youth continued on many days over the mountains and through valleys. To the Senecas courage and perseverance were the greatest virtues. He became very tired and sat down to rest on a mountaintop and saw a little house in a valley below. Perhaps he could find some information about the bear trail. Like many heroes, he was following his path, his destiny. He was caught by this trail without knowing where it led. Many discoveries occur in just this unconscious way. Any significant life is just such a journey, a pilgrimage into the future toward the east where the sun rises, toward the unknown.

Soon he reached the cabin and found a woman and her five daughters grinding corn on metates. Finally the feminine element emerges in the tale. Only the women know where the bear trail leads. Men can seldom achieve much unless they recognize and listen to the feminine within them. Men who do not integrate their feminine side are lopsided human beings. All numbers have meaning, which has intrigued men and women from the dawn of time. The great mathematician, Kurt Gödel, showed that numbers have a life of their own. There are five daughters. Five is a number of completeness, for the quintessence of a matter.

The youth meets wholeness grinding the corn, sacramental to the Natives of North America. This was a holy scene! One of the daughters spoke up and gave him directions. He must cross many more mountains and valleys (symbolic of difficulties that one encounters on the hero's way) and then he will find another house in a valley. Those living there will be able to tell him where the path leads. Our young man is a seeker, and persistent seekers often find more than they are looking for. They even find redemption that they never dreamed could be theirs. The angels who come to rescue Faust from Satan's grasp are singing, "those whose seeking never ceases are ours for their redeeming."

At last he saw a log cabin in a valley. The door was open; nothing was being hidden from his seeking, and he was welcome. How inviting is the open door to those who make either the outer or the inner journey. Again we find a woman and her five daughters. He asks for help. We seldom get help when we do not ask for it. One line of a poem of Rumi reads, "You must ask for what you really want." The young man was told that he was nearly at his goal. One more mountain to the east, another valley, and on top of the next mountain he would find a little house; there the trail ends.

Energized, he hurries toward his goal. He approaches the log cabin. An old man totters out of the house. With a cry of welcome, the aged one speaks, "My son, my son, you have come back to me." The boy is bewildered, but his father leads him into the house and tells him that he had been captured by his father's enemy who is not really his uncle. This is the man who raised him, but he is a dangerous and powerful man who can transform himself into a bear. He is a negative shaman-witch. He will know where the youth has journeyed. We are often captives of the subconscious without knowing it.

The boy and his father must prepare for the bear-uncle immediately. The youth is sent to collect splinters of pine wood. The father also has magical power. Indeed, nearly all of these charaters have unusual spiritual powers. These stories suggest that all of us may have more power than we realize. The father commands the house to get smaller and smaller so that the great bear can get only his paw inside the door. The house shrinks; the enemy comes; the bear sticks its paw in and lighted splinters of pine are thrust into it. The oily bear catches fire. He runs for water, but instead of a pond, he jumps into an oil well and is consumed.

One of the most sacred places in the original Seneca country was an area with oil springs and ponds; this area is still a reservation belonging to the Seneca nation. The witch was destroyed by fire; at the very same time Europeans were disposing of witches in the same way.

The father then ordered the house to return to its former size. The lost had been found, the captive had been set free, the enemy had been destroyed, father and son had been reunited, the value and helpfulness of the feminine had been acknowledged and used. The boy probably married one of the ten daughters and life continued on. Evil has been conquered again. The Great Spirit has been victorious again because of human courage and faith.

TWO MORE CAPTIVES

We are not told whether the story of the two captives refers to a raid among Iroquois tribes before the Iroquois confederacy or to capture by a hostile band of a more distant marauding tribe. Incessant warfare among various Indian tribes plagued a great number of Native Americans. This was more a game with high risks than modern Western warfare. It was for this reason that the Five Nations were such a remarkable exception. A tribe went out on the warpath. One of the main purposes of this game-like warfare was to take captives, either to fill in their own depleted ranks, or to kill or torture members of an enemy tribe in retaliation for what had been done to them. Warfare was also engaged in for the fun of it. This was one of the less attractive qualities of ancient Native American life. Today's tribes are countries and today's warfare is infinitely more destructive with explosives and "smart bombs."

A great feast was held and a large fire was made. When the fire had burned down to coals, the captive warriors were told to walk through the coals. Two of the captives were then told to run a race after this torture. Since the captives spoke another tongue they could talk to one another without being understood. They made their plans carefully. As they ran the gauntlet between the crowds (the same kind of people who watched the gladiators and the witchburnings and executions in Europe), they would jump over their captors' heads and disappear into the forest. Again, before we are too critical of these spectators, we need to look at ourselves and see the sadistic side that lies deep within most of us. In California thirty years ago, a well-known criminal was executed in the gas chamber and the event was broadcast over the radio. In one junior college classroom, everything stopped as students listened to the last gasps of the dying man. If executions were still public, large crowds would undoubtedly still gather to watch them just as they watched Jesus and the two men crucified with him die on their crosses. Some of the pleasure we find in the more violent sports may be in watching another (enemy) person or team knocked about.

Imagine these woodsmen running with corn kernels stuck into the soft flesh beneath the leather-like soles of their feet. They ran, they jumped, and fled. Night came. The captives ran on and then jumped into a river. During the day they hid beneath the overhanging banks of the river. Being very clever as well as very courageous men, they swam nearly submerged, making sounds like the quacking of ducks. In one place a group of people was camping by the river. Someone in the group threw a bone to scare the ducks away and struck one man in the mouth, knocking out his teeth. At last these men reached their tribe and were welcomed with great joy. Their feet healed, but one man was without teeth the rest of his life. Victory came at last to these two warrior-heroes.

The Seneca youth and boys who heard this tale were given a lesson in what it meant to be a warrior: stoic, Spartan endurance of pain, the courage to survive capture, and the wisdom and ingenuity necessary to use their courage wisely. The same courage and wisdom are required by those who are captured by darkness, disillusionment, and meaninglessness. Only the persistent, courageous, and astute make it through. These captives also had one another. Would they have made it alone? Often we need a companion if we are to escape our inner captivity and come home.

CHAPTER TEN

Haton-dos, The Listener

Haton-dos and his uncle lived together in a hut. When Haton-dos was a small boy, his uncle said to him one day, "You are now old enough to go into the woods and listen. Go today and listen. Then come and tell me what you hear."

The boy went outdoors. Soon he returned and said that he had heard something that made a strange sound. He made the sound and his uncle said, "That was a chickadee."

The next day Haton-dos went again into the woods. He listened. When he came home he repeated to his uncle the sound he had heard. The uncle said, "That is a bobolink."

Another time he heard a noise that frightened him. When he tried to make the same noise, his uncle said, "That was a bear."

Each day Haton-dos heard new sounds and learned about the bird or animal to which the sound belonged. For years he went out, pressing deeper and deeper into the woods and learning the voices of birds and animals.

At last, one day he heard a song on a distant hazy line of mountains to the west. Someone was singing. It was the sweetest sound he had ever heard. Haton-dos told his uncle of this new voice. His uncle said, "That is the voice of a woman. Listen to it tomorrow, for you will hear it again."

The next morning Haton-dos heard the song and he saw the woman. She was singing and the song was: "Haton-dos, I am coming to be your wife. My mother is with me. I am her youngest daughter. Haton-dos, I am coming to be your wife. My mother is with me. I am her youngest daughter.

Haton-dos, I am coming to be your wife. My mother is with me. I am her youngest daughter."

Haton-dos was a good runner. He hurried back and told his uncle. The uncle said, "I have seen the old woman and her daughter in their canoe. They are searching for 'The Listener.' This canoe of theirs is used on dry land or in the air. You must prepare for the coming of your wife. The daughter and her mother are coming here. This was the object of your listening."

Haton-dos put on his coat of skins and his leggings with fringe down the sides. He tried on several suits. His uncle looked at each suit and had him change until he was well-fitted and looked his best. Then the uncle said, "You must be very careful, for the old woman is a harsh, rough woman. She has a number of tricks for you to go through." And after Haton-dos was ready to leave, his uncle said to him, "Go toward the east to meet the canoe."

Haton-dos ran toward the east to the place where he expected to meet the woman. He missed them. When he found that they were not there, the Listener pulled a horn out of his belt. He stuck it in the ground and pulled it back and forth. It gathered up the distance into a few steps. He overtook the women. He said to the old woman, "I have come for your daughter."

The old woman's name was De-ga-us-ka-u-da-you. She said, "Many young men are after my daughters. I have nine other daughters. You, Haton-dos, are the tenth man." When night came, they made a camp. The old woman said, "How are we going to get our supper?"

Haton-dos said to the other men, "How are we going to get it?"

They said, "We don't know, but since De-ga-us-ka-u-da-you demanded it, we must get it some way."

They started out in search of something to eat. At last they came to where a tree had blown over. There they found a bear. A man who had a hammer struck through the tree, killed the bear, and they dressed it. They carried it to camp. They had supper together and then the men went to sleep.

When the men were asleep the old woman took all the men's clothing away. She called for a high tree to bend over. The tree bent over and she put all the clothes of the men on the treetop.

In the morning when the men awoke, the women were gone. They could not find their clothes. Then they saw them hanging on the treetop. The Listener called for the tree to bend over. The tree brought back the clothes. The men dressed. One of the men was in a hurry to overtake the women. The other nine men took a long time to dress. They said, "Never mind the women. Don't be in a hurry."

The women traveled in a canoe in the air, paddling as if they were in the water. They went very fast. When the men were ready, the boy gathered up the land with his horn. The women thought they had gone a long way ahead of the men. They were surprised when the men caught up to them this time. Haton-dos and the nine men went and found supper without being asked.

At nighttime, when the women were asleep, Haton-dos took the women's clothing and their canoe. He put the clothes into the canoe and called to a high tree to bend over. The tree bent over. Haton-dos placed the canoe with the clothes in it on the treetop. He threw ashes toward the treetop and said, "No one and nothing can climb this tree."

Snow began to fall and the ground froze. The men shivered.

They moved on and camped. When the women awoke and found that their clothes and canoe were gone, De-ga-us-ka-u-da-you said, "I am going to be a bat." She turned into a bat and flew and flew, but she couldn't reach the canoe. Then one of the daughters said, "I will be a flying squirrel." She became a flying squirrel, but she could not reach the treetop. They began to cry, "O Listener! Have mercy on us. Come back. Come back. O Listener! Have mercy on us. Come back. Come back. O Listener! Have mercy on us. Come back. Come back."

So the Listener came back. He made the women promise not to play any more tricks. When they had promised, the Listener called to the tree to bend over. He gave the clothes to the women. As soon as they were dressed, De-ga-us-ka-u-da-you and her daughters wished to go on, but the Listener said, "I want something to eat before I go on. You must get it for me."

So they furnished him with bear meat. The other nine men had started ahead, but they were in no hurry because they depended on the Listener.

Before they reached the home of De-ga-us-ka-u-da-you, they came to a mountain of ice. No man could climb this mountain. If he tried, he always slid back. The women had their canoe. They paddled through the air and reached the top of the mountain. The nine men tried to climb the mountain of ice, but they slid back. The Listener did not try.

At last he said, "I am going to walk over. If you men are going to follow me, look nowhere except where I step. When you get near the top the old woman, De-ga-us-ka-u-da-you, will call, 'Here you are! How fine-looking you are! Just see how fine-looking this is that I have near me.' But don't look. If you do look, you will fall dead."

Then Haton-dos went to his bundle which he carried with him and took from it a red robin. He put the robin on his head. He shook his head. The robin came to life. Haton-dos said to the robin, "Sing!" and the robin sang. As the robin sang, the ice began to melt. At every step the Listener took, there was a foothold. The men followed in his steps. When they were near the top of the mountain, they heard the old woman clapping her hands. She walked back and forth and called, "Here they come. Here they come. How fine-looking they are! Here they come. Here they come. How fine-looking they are!"

The men did not look. They reached the top of the mountain safely. The Listener told the men not to look at the house at the top of the hill. He said, "You must pay no attention to what the old woman says. If you do, sudden death will come to you."

Then the men started down the hill on the other side. The red robin kept singing. The men could hear the old woman, who had now gone to the foot of the hill. She was clapping her hands. Little bells were tied to her wrists. She was saying, "Here they come. Here they come. See what a pleasant home we have!"

The Listener led the way. Each man stepped where the Listener stepped, for the ice was melting. All at once they heard something fall behind them, rattle, rattle, and slip by them. It was the bones of one of the men who was weak-minded. He had no courage and he looked. The nine men who remained kept on until they reached the foot of the mountain, where the house of the old woman was.

The house of the old woman was made of bark. It had ten fireplaces, one for each of the ten daughters. Each daughter was to have a man, but the man who was to be the husband of the oldest daughter had looked and his bones had rattled down the hill. At quite a distance from the house of the women was another house. The old woman took the men there. It was built of ice. De-ga-us-ka-u-da-you said to the men, "Go inside of the house. Sit down on the seats which are there."

They went inside. The Listener said to the men, "Don't sit down. We can stand awhile. If you sit down, you will die."

In a short time, the old woman came into the house and said, "I will bring you something to eat."

When she left, she closed the door. The men could not tell where the door was. It froze into the rest of the ice around it. The Listener began to sing his song. The bird sang. The ice began to melt. All at once, the door opened. The old woman and one daughter brought in a large brass kettle filled with hominy.

De-ga-us-ka-u-da-you said, "There are dried apples in the hominy."

They were really live leeches instead. When she and her daughter left, she closed the door. She thought that the men were safely imprisoned and that they would be poisoned by the leeches and die. She did not notice that the ice was melting. The men were still standing. The Listener pulled out a tube from his bow and arrow. He swallowed the tube. He ate the hominy. It ran through the tube under the benches.

The Listener said, "I can eat anything De-ga-us-ka-u-da-you brings me. You must eat nothing or you will die."

The Listener threw the kettle against the side of the house. The old woman heard it and came in with another kettle. This one was full of soup. The Listener said, "Thank you for your kindness. I see that we are not likely to be hungry."

He noticed something that clicked against the side of the brass kettle. It looked like flint stone and it seemed to be alive. The old woman closed the door when she left. The Listener drank the soup. It went through him and did not harm him. By the time he had emptied the brass kettle, the men could see through the roof of the building, for it had melted.

De-ga-us-ka-u-da-you came after the brass kettle. She did not notice how thin the roof had become. The Listener walked about the room and the bird kept singing. The ice melted faster and faster. Soon the men had no walls around them. Then they were taken to the house which was made of bark where the old woman and her ten daughters lived.

When they were in the house made of bark, De-ga-us-ka-u-da-you told each man which of her daughters should be his wife. The youngest daughter was given to the Listener. The next youngest daughter was given to the man who was next bravest to the Listener. He was called "Hammer-handle-through-his-hip," for he had a hammer handle right through his hip.

Night came. Everybody went to bed. The bed in the farthest part of the room was the old woman's bed. Not long after dark she had a horrible dream. She arose in her sleep and rolled around on the floor, into the fire, here and there. The noise awakened the Listener. He said, "What is the matter, Mother-in-law? Wake up!"

Hammer-handle-through-his-hip was also awake. He drew out his hammer and struck the old woman on her head. She awoke and said, "I am awake. Don't strike me any more."

The Listener said, "What did you dream?"

She answered, "I dreamed that you went to the lake and killed a red otter."

The Listener thought, "If she dreads to have me kill the red otter, I think I had better kill it." When he had a chance, he asked his wife, "What is the red otter?"

She said, "The red otter is my mother's husband."

The Listener said to De-ga-us-ka-u-da-you, "I am going to kill the red otter."

His wife said, "If you go, I will be fair with you. While you are gone, the east door of the house must be kept moving or you will die."

The next morning he prepared to go to the lake to kill the red otter. The Listener told Hammer-handle-through-his-hip to watch the door. The Listener fastened one end of a line to his leg. The other end he fastened to the door. This line was able to stretch and become very long. As the Listener walked, his leg kept moving the string and the string kept the door moving. The Listener told Hammer-handle-through-his-hip to keep the old woman from closing the door so that it could not move.

Then the Listener left and went east. He came to a very large lake. He reached the lake by going through a ravine. When he reached the edge of the lake he said, "You who live in this lake, come out! I want you. You who live in this lake, come out! I want you."

All at once the water was stirred up, Many water animals came out. Among them was a white otter, but no red otter. The Listener said to the white otter, "I don't want you. I want a red one." The animals disappeared into the water. The white otter sank into the water, and a red one came to the surface.

The Listener said to the red otter, "Come to the shore!" The red otter came to the shore and the Listener killed it. As soon as he had killed it, the Listener began to skin and dress the animal and to chop the flesh into fine pieces. By the time he had chopped the flesh and tied it up to carry it away, the water began to rise. The Listener ran for his life with the otter on his shoulder. Once, on the way, the water struck his heel and it became raw to the bone. He kept running up the ravine towards high ground, and he ran until he came to a place where the water stopped rising. The Listener spit on his fingers, rubbed his heel with the spit, and it was made well again.

When the Listener returned home, he untied his bundle, put the flesh into a kettle, and boiled it. De-ga-us-ka-u-da-you was very anxious to get a small piece of the meat.

But the Listener said, "You keep away! You cannot have any."

When it was cooked, he called for the Giant-False-Faces who lived in the woods. The Listener invited two of the Giant-False-Faces to eat the feast he had prepared. These two Giant-False-Faces came and rattled on the door with mud turtle shells. They came into the house. They took paddles and danced around the kettle and sang. After the two Giant-False-Faces danced, they went to the kettle which was full of meat and soup, and they ate every bit of it. This feast lasted nearly all night. When the Giant-False-Faces went home, the men went to sleep.

In the morning they went outdoors to see what was around

them. At the foot of the hill they saw heaps of human bones. There were many old bones covered with mold and moss. The men were astonished that so many people had been killed as they came over the mountain. No one knew how long De-ga-us-ka-u-da-you had been killing men by enticing them to look.

As the men walked, they came to a large open field. The men walked around and did nothing but look all the day. When night came, they went to bed. It was not long before the old woman began dreaming horrible dreams. She arose and tumbled around on the floor. The Listener got up. He took her by the hair and pulled her around.

He said, "What is the matter, Mother-in-law? Wake up!"

She awoke. He asked her what her dream was.

She said, "I dreamed that you went and killed a large bird that inhabits the clouds. It is king of all the birds. It is a rare bird and is seldom seen." De-ga-us-ka-u-da-you pointed to the direction in which the bird lived.

She said, "He lives in the top of a big elm tree. I dreamed that you killed it and brought it to the house. I think you can't do it."

The Listener said, "I can kill the bird easily enough." When the Listener was alone with his wife, he asked her what this bird was.

She said, "It is my mother's oldest son." The Listener prepared to go to kill the bird.

Before he started, the old woman said, "I will be fair with you. The door must be kept moving. It must rattle. I will try to stop it."

The Listener said to Hammer-handle-through-his-hip, "You let De-ga-us-ka-u-da-you get hold of the door once in a while. She will soon find out that she will suffer for it. But you keep the door rattling." Then the Listener left and went to the place where the big elm tree stood. There was a large nest in the treetop.

He said, "Tree, bend over so I can take the bird from its nest." The tree bent over. It came toward him where he stood. When it was in just the right position, he took his spear and speared the bird. The bird was almost as tall as he was. The Listener commenced to pick the feathers from the bird and to pull the flesh to pieces and bundle it up. When it was ready to carry, he put it on his back. He went back to the house. All the while he was gone, he held onto the hook and line which kept the door moving. The old woman tried to stop the door, but the door pinched her fingers so that they bled.

Hammer-handle-through-his-hip said to her, "That is what you get for trying to close the door. You will lose your hand if you don't look out." Then she left the door alone.

When the Listener returned to the house, he said to his mother-in-law, "I have killed the bird and now I will cook it." He prepared the kettle, put the flesh and the feathers into the kettle, and put it over the fire to boil. The old woman wanted a piece of the flesh or even a feather.

But the Listener said, "No! You can't have any." She cried. She knew if she could get even a bit of flesh or a feather, she could bring the big bird back to life again.

After the bird was cooked, the Listener invited the two Giant-False-Faces to eat the feast. They came, one at the east door and one at the west door. Both Giant-False-Faces knocked with mud turtle shells. They danced around the kettle and ate up everything. After dancing and eating, the Giant-False-Faces went back into the woods where they belonged. It was near daylight when the Giant-False-Faces disappeared. The old woman, her daughters, and sons-in-laws didn't sleep much that night.

During the next day, the men traveled here and there about the country. While they were gone, the youngest daughter said to her mother, "You have the wrong man this time. He is going to destroy us all. I have often told you that you have done very wrong deeds. I think we are going to get our pay for our wickedness this time. We will all be killed."

Night came. The Listener went to bed quite early, before the others. Soon he had a horrible dream. He jumped and rolled around as his mother-in-law had done. She went and took the corn pounder and knocked him on the head. He said, "I am awake," but she struck him again. After he was wide awake, De-ga-us-ka-u-da-you said, "What dream did you have?"

He said, "That is for you to find out."

Then she commenced guessing his dream. When she could not guess it, she called her daughters to guess.

He said, "If you cannot guess my dream by morning, you will all die." Then they guessed and guessed until almost daylight.

When it was morning, the Listener said, "You have failed to guess my dream. I warned you that death would come." He then called his men outside and he made the women stay inside.

He said, "Let this house turn into stone and let the doors be fastened into the stone." The house, with the women closed inside, turned to stone. Then the men circled around the house and sang. The red robin sat on the Listener's hat and sang.

The men sang, "De-ga-us-ka-u-da-you, misfortune to you at daybreak! De-ga-us-ka-u-da-you, misfortune to you at daybreak! De-ga-us-ka-u-da-you, misfortune to you at daybreak!" While they sang, the men walked around and around the long house and the house began to get red hot. The women cried for mercy.

"Let us out! Let us out!" The Listener's wife called him by name.

He said, "No, you cannot come out."

She said, "There is one important thing I want to tell you."

Hammer-handle-through-his-hip said, "Listener, you'd better let her out." The Listener opened the door and let his wife out, but he kept the others in. They were hot and miserable. Finally they died because of the heat. The head of De-ga-us-ka-u-da-you, burst open and an owl came out and flew away through the chimney. The daughters came out as screech owls, foxes, and other poor worthless animals. That was the last of the woman who traveled all over the country and hunted for husbands for her daughters in order to kill men.

In the morning the Listener said to his companions, "Gather up the bones which are piled at the foot of the hill and put a tepee over the bone heap." When they had done this, the Listener went to the tree nearest the tepee and kicked the tree so that it fell towards the tepee.

He called out, "Look out for your lives!" The bones all came to life. The men saw their companion who had slipped by them on the hill a few days before.

The Listener said to the people, "Go home where you belong." Some of the men did not know where their homes were, because it had been so long since they left them that they had forgotten. He told them to go home with the other men, and he told his own companions to return to their own homes. It is said of the Listener's friend, Hammer-handle-through-his-hip, that when you hear the frost cracking in winter, you may know that it is Hammer-handle-through-his-hip who is striking the trees.

When the men had departed, the Listener, with his wife, started towards the east. He asked her what was the important thing she wished to tell him.

She said, "I have a young brother. No one knows about him and no one ever went to see him but me." While they were talking, they came to a swamp. It seemed like grass, but it was a bog. Trees grew all around. She stepped here and there in the swamp. The Listener stood on the edge of the swamp. His wife disappeared momentarily, but soon came into sight again. She had a very small young deer in her arms. The deer was spotted. She gave it to her husband. He put it on the framework of bark which he had on his back. They went on together.

His wife said to him, "I want to warn you about a place where you will hear women singing. The house where the women are is a longhouse, and the road goes through the middle of it. The women sit in the house on each side of the road. You must close your eyes. If you open them, you will be blind."

They walked on towards the east. They had not gone far when the Listener began to think that his wife was useless to him. He thought he might as well destroy her, too, as he had her mother and sisters. He knew she could tell him nothing more that was important. When he had decided to get rid of her, he gave her a sudden push. She fell upon the ground, dead. She turned into a duck, and that was the last of his wife.

The Listener traveled alone. He had the deer and his bow and arrows on his shoulder. He always found bountiful game on his journey. He traveled a long time; it might have been months. He walked the road or path where people always traveled back and forth. After a long time, one day he heard women singing.

When he came to the house, the women called, "Look at her! See how beautiful she is. Look at her! Look at her! See how beautiful she is. Look at her!" He closed his eyes as he was going through the gauntlet of women. Two of the women followed him. They said, "Look at us! Look at us!" He was only in the doorway, but he thought he was outside. He looked. The women had a quilt which was made of buckskin. It was covered with eyes. When the Listener looked, his eyes fell out upon the buckskin and he was blind. The women took his bow and arrows, and his deer ran away from him. He went on, but he did not know where to go because he was blind.

He lost his way. He grew hungry. He did not know what to do. He felt the bushes and found leaves which tasted good. They were buck leaves. He lived on the buck leaves and drank from the brooks. He knew when night came because most of the birds stopped singing then, and whistlers started whistling at twilight. When the birds began to whistle, he knew night was coming, and when all the birds began to sing he knew it was morning. All he could tell was when it was day and when it was night. He traveled nearly all summer through the woods until his clothes were torn off by the bushes.

One day while he was traveling, it seemed to him that he came to a cornfield. By feeling the leaves he found the corn and ate it. Then he thought that people must live nearby or the corn would not be growing there. He decided to go where he could be seen. It was not long before he heard someone coming, but whoever it was went away again.

The cornfield belonged to a young woman and her mother who lived by themselves. It was the young woman whom the Listener had heard. When the girl saw the Listener, she wondered at the strange sight. She went home and told her mother what she had seen. The mother said, "We will go and see what it is." So they went to where the Listener stood. The old woman approached him, took his hand, and said, "It is a man."

Then she knew he had been through the house where they take away the eyes of men. The woman took the Listener home and washed and fed him and said, "We are very fortunate. It seems to us that he is a brave man."

That day the old woman said to her daughter, "Go to the cornfield and scare away the crows."

The Listener said, "I will go. They will be afraid of me because of the way I look." He insisted on going and said, "Have you a bow and arrow?" The old woman hunted up a very old and smoky bow and one arrow. The Listener said,

"Take me over to the cornfield." So they took him there. He said, "Take me to the further end of the field next to the woods." There he was taken, and he leaned up against the stump of a tree. The women left him and went home to their work. As he stood there, he heard a rattling in the leaves that sounded like something dragging itself through the corn and eating it. He drew up his bow and arrow. He listened closely, and then shot. The corn stalks rattled and away the animal went. He listened, but could not tell what it was.

After a time the women came and he said, "I shot something in that direction." The girl went in search and found a very large deer with the arrow straight through its body. The Listener had listened well. He knew his business. The women were very glad. The girl went to the house for a knife, and the mother began to skin the deer.

The Listener said, "Wait a minute! Pull out its eyes. Maybe I can see with them." It was true, for when he put the deer's eyes in his own sockets, he could see fairly well.

He took the knife and skinned the deer. After he was through and the deer was cut up, he helped carry it to the house. Both of the women liked the man and wanted him to stay with them.

The next day he said, "I am going to hunt." He went beyond the cornfield into the woods. Not far from the cornfield, he saw an elk and shot it. He skinned and dressed it and carried to the house all the hide and meat that he could. It was a very large elk, and the Listener could not carry all of it. The women went and brought home the rest of the meat. The old woman thought that the Listener must belong to a good family, because he had magic power and was very brave.

The next day he could see but dimly. Then he went to the cornfield and watched until a deer came to eat corn. He could see only the outline of the deer. He shot and killed the deer and dragged the body to the house. When he got there the first thing he did was pull out the deer's eyes, throw away the ones he had used, and put in the new ones. Then he could see better.

Finally the old woman told her daughter that she had better be this man's wife. She said to her daughter, "He goes hunting nearby every day." After he felt at home, the Listener took the young girl for his wife. He kept changing his eyes. This was the only way he could see.

In about a year a child was born. The old woman threw the baby into the woodshed. Another baby was born. The babies were twins. The grandmother named the firstborn, Burnt-belly, and the second-one, Scorched-body. Soon the boys began to play, peeping through the door and laughing. They grew very, very fast. The second day, the children crept into the room where their mother was. The grandmother did not want them to live, and this was why she had thrown them into the wood-shed. When they crept through the door, she scolded them and said, "You must go back. You cannot come in here." But they came in, laughing. Their mother took them into her lap.

One of the boys pointed to his father and said, "What is that?"

She said, "That is your father." Then they knew that they had a father.

The boys grew fast. The next day they came in again. One boy asked his mother, "What happened to father's eyes?" She told the boys, for she knew what had happened to her husband when he came through the house of the women. The boys went back to the woodshed and talked together.

The elder boy said, "We will go after those eyes." The boys had magic power. They went underground. They came out close to the place where the women were singing. When they were near, they made this plan. The older boy said, "There is a spring nearby where the women go to get water. You go there and become a little duck. I will watch. After you become a little duck, someone with a pail will come for water. She will chase you around, going back and forth, and you enter her womb. In a few days she will give birth to a child. You must cry. Do not stop crying until they wrap you in the buckskin blanket which is covered with eyes."

After this was planned, the boys went to the spring and the younger one did as his brother told him. It happened just as he had planned, and a child was born. It was a beautiful boy and all the women loved him. Oh, how they loved him. But he cried and cried. The women carried him by turns, but they could not stop his crying.

At last one woman said, "We must wrap him in the buckskin blanket." A smile came upon the baby's face. So they wrapped him in the blanket, and he pretended to be asleep. The women were worn out with his crying. When they thought he was asleep, they went to sleep. Then the baby returned to its form as a boy. He arose and said, "Let everyone in this house sleep as if dead." So they slept.

The boy carried the buckskin blanket which was covered with eyes to his brother. The boys looked over all the eyes and selected the freshest looking ones for their father. Then they thought, "While our father was traveling, he must have had something he was carrying." So they went into the house and searched. They found the young deer on the bark frame. The frame leaned against the wall. Then they found his bow and arrows. They chose those which had the least dust on them.

Then the boys set the whole building on fire and burned all the women and all the things the women had in the house. The brothers returned home by an underground passageway. They took the buckskin blanket, the deer, and the bow and arrows.

All at once the Listener, his wife, and mother-in-law heard the children laughing outside. They were glad, for the boys had been gone several days and they had missed them. The boys went into the house. They had the buckskin blanket wrapped wrong side out. They said to their father, "Father, look here, we have your eyes. Wait just a moment."

Then they put his own eyes in his sockets, and this was the first time he knew just what his boys looked like. After the father had his eyes and all the family was happy, the boys said to their parents, "We are going all over the world. We are going to destroy everything that is bad. We are going to put out of the world everything that destroys human life."

After they had gone and the Listener was alone, he had time to think. One day he remembered his uncle with whom he had lived when he was a boy. He remembered that his uncle had told him when he left home, "When you get in trouble, think of me. I will help you." All these years, when he lost his eyes and had every trouble, the Listener had forgotten this promise. While the Listener was thinking of this, suddenly his uncle appeared before him as though he came out of the ground. The uncle remained. After destroying the evil in the world, the boys came home, and the uncle, the Listener, the wife, mother-in-law, and sons of the Listener lived together in peace and joy forever.

CHAPTER ELEVEN

The Adventures of an Enchanted Hero

In the story of Haton-dos, we enter fully and deeply into the enchanted world of the Senecas and also into the culture and pulsating life of primal religion. Although little is said about the creation myth, the story assumes a knowledge of Seneca religious life. Before I knew the basic Iroquois religious beliefs, I did not understand this story.

In several places we encounter the Giant-False-Faces who were described earlier. The name of these spiritual powers is capitalized. These powers were the manifestation of the omnipresent defeated evil spirit and could represent either the original Evil Brother himself, or his multiple manifestations as forest spirits, or the masks that Seneca men made and wore in their sacred dances and ceremonies. The triple significance of these figures is characteristic of primal religion. As we enter this world we also step into what Jung calls the collective unconscious, what is referred to by some writers as the intermediate spiritual world. This domain contains both the angelic and demonic powers and is distinguished from the divine world of the creating Loving Holy One in many religions.[1]

Haton-dos was living with his uncle in typical matrilineal fashion. The uncle has supernatural power. He has foreknowledge of what will happen and the trials through which his nephew must pass before he attains full development and a satisfactory life. The boy's training began when he was very young. The boy was told to go out into the forest and to listen and then return and describe the sounds that he heard. For those who lived in the forest, learning to listen was important, a matter of life or death.

As the boy grew to manhood he became so skilled in his ability to distinguish different sounds that he was named the Listener. One day on a distant hazy mountain he heard a new sound, the sweetest sound that he had ever heard. When he described this to his uncle, the older man replied that he had heard the song of a woman and he was to go out and listen again the next day. Three times he heard the song.

His uncle had been waiting for this time. He knew of the woman and her daughter and their magical canoe. He knew that they were searching for the Listener. He also knew that this young man must learn to deal with both the outer woman and his own inner woman if he were to become the hero he could become. The uncle also warned him that the old woman was harsh, and he would have to go through many trials before he would be able to marry this young woman. His training in listening was part of his preparation for the dangers and diffi-culties of his journey. Then he told his nephew that a man seeking a wife must be properly dressed. Haton-dos had to try on many different deerskin suits before he could set out to the east to meet the canoe and his future wife.

No detail in a dream or myth is unimportant, particularly those which may seem most insignificant. The young man must be wearing the wedding garment if he is to enter the feast of the kingdom of wholeness. Native Americans in an unknown part of the world were using the same symbols that Jesus used in his parables. One reason that the parables of Jesus still strike home is that he used the archetypal symbols of the soul. Our clothing is what covers our nakedness and vulnerability; clothing can represent our learned way of protecting us from the elements and our manner of presenting ourselves to the world.

Dreams of nakedness usually mean that we are naive and think that people will take us just as we are. A psychiatrist friend told me that he could usually tell a person who was psychotic just by the way he or she dressed. Some people never learn to put on appropriate clothing, the proper attitude for different occasions. Others identify with their clothing and become the masks they wear. I am writing this on a ship where clothes are very important; personas are very well polished and keep people from much real communication. Uniforms are used to unify diverse people or to indicate rank. Those who go on the journey to the holy marriage need to know themselves well, and at the same time must learn how to present themselves to the world.

Once properly attired with the appropriate attitude, the uncle told the Listener to call if he ever needed help and the uncle would come. The Listener ran toward the east; in nearly every one of these tales travel is toward the east. The women and their flying canoe had gone on and so he took out a magic horn, placed it in the earth, and pulled it back and forth. This action gathered up the ground between him and the women and he was able to overtake them. The horn was for Haton-dos what the seven league boots were for the hero in that fairytale.

But why the horn? In many cultures the horn was a symbol of power. Many of the Greek gods were horned and so were many of their heroes. For the Israelites, the horns of the altar were sacred and Moses had horns. The horn is also a symbol of fertility and the cornucopia of plenty. It is both a masculine and a feminine symbol, one of both penetration and receptivity. The one who owns such a horn is indeed a person of power. This symbol is predictive of Haton-dos' ultimate success.

Our hero announced to the old woman that he had come for her youngest daughter. He was told that he was the tenth man. Nine other men had already come for her other daughters. Ten is another number of completeness in many cultures, a symbol of perfection and finality. There are ten commandments, ten spheres of heaven, ten words in Cabala by which God created the world, ten fingers and ten toes. Pythagorians saw ten as the symbol of the wonders of the world, the number that was more important than all others. This story is about wholeness, and promises a final, creative solution at its end. But Haton-dos must be as patient as Pilgrim in Bunyan's *Pilgrim's Progress*.

Now that the tenth man has been found, the plot of the story can unfold. The old woman asked the men how all twenty-one of them were going to eat that evening. The men consulted with each other and then went hunting. They found a bear in a hollow tree that had fallen over. These stories are filled with hollow trees; hollow trees large enough to hide a bear would be a great rarity in Seneca country. Along with superhuman heroes we have supernatural trees. From the creation myth we know that the world tree, falling out of heaven, created the earth. The tree stands for the axis that connects heaven and earth. In Chinese thought, there are not four elements, but five: earth, air, fire, water, and wood. To the Senecas, the trees are as alive as human beings and animals and stones. The Great Mother, Isis, hid Osiris in a wooden box from which he was resurrected. Through this hollow tree, nature has provided an answer to the men's problem — a bear, the only animal that could feed all of them, and the best of food as well. Only a monumental and magical hollow tree could hide a bear.

When they had all eaten and were asleep, the old woman was up to her tricks. One of these living trees responded to her command and bent over. She placed in its highest branches the clothing that she had collected from the men during their sleep. When the men awoke, the women had left in their canoe, paddling through the air. This way of travel reminds one of the witches flying on their broomsticks. The Listener was a man of power, too, and he simply commanded the tree to bend over and it obeyed. One man was in a great hurry to get dressed so they could follow the women, but the others gave very sage advice, "Never mind the women. Don't be in a hurry." As we have already seen in another story, haste can cause disaster.

Haton-dos' horn was as powerful as the women's canoe. I am sure that Freud would have seen sexual symbolism in the canoe and the horn. The magic horn brings the men quickly to where the women had sped away. Again, the men provided game for supper.

The contest between the magicians, Haton-dos and De-ga-us-ka-u-da-you, continued. After the women were asleep, the Listener ordered a tall tree to bend over and he placed in its branches not only the women's clothing, but their canoe as well. Then he threw ashes toward the treetop and pronounced a charm that made it impossible for anyone to climb the tree. Then, as in our first story, the snow began to fall and the men moved on. I have been able to find no similar symbol of ashes creating snow in other mythology. Usually ashes represent fire or cleansing. Sometimes symbols can represent their opposites, or it may be that ashes resemble snow. Ashes may be to fire as snow is to absence of the sun and warmth. The women were powerless to get back their possession even though the old woman turned herself into a bat (an ominous symbol of darkness and evil) and one of the daughters became a flying squirrel.

At last they were forced to call on Haton-dos for help. He returned, although one wonders why he would return after all this trickery. However, the hero has to deal with the negative aspects of the feminine before he can find its positive nature. The Listener made the women promise to play no more tricks on them. As we have seen, the promises of either male or female witches cannot be relied upon. The hero then took a stand and would not let them go until the women provided them some bear meat for their meal.

The ten men then came to a mountain of ice that separated them from the women they were seeking. Few ordinary human beings can climb over a wall of ice. In Dante's *Inferno*, Satan is frozen in a cake of ice in the very center of the earth. Ice can represent the dividing line between consciousness and the unconcious. In dreams it often refers to a lack of human warmth and sexual feeling. Here it is a glacier-like barrier that keeps the band of seekers from their goal.

Haton-dos is telepathic and knew what the old woman would do. He instructed his companions to step only in his footsteps. When they got to the top of the mountain they must not look at the Medusa-like old woman or they would drop dead. Then he took out his medicine bundle, his leather bag of power charms. From it he extracted a red robin, the symbol of spring and of the airy good spirits. He attached the robin to his head and commanded it to sing. The robin came to life, the mountain of ice began to melt, and the men were able to follow in the steps of their master. They had just started down the other side when they heard something fall rattling down behind them — the bones of a weak-minded man who could not keep from looking.

Weak-mindedness, the inability to follow because of a lack of inner discipline, ranked at the top of the hierarchy of Iroquois vices.

The old woman and her daughters were living in a typical

Seneca longhouse where members of extended families had lived
for generations. These longhouses were made of bark tied to a
wooden frame. They were often more than sixty feet long and
about thirty feet wide. Each little family unit had its own space
for storing possessions and a fireplace and a smoke hole in the
roof above it. The ceremonial longhouses of the followers of
Handsome Lake and "the old way" are still built on the same
plan, but they have only one smoke hole or chimney in the
middle of the building. When the men approached the longhouse, they were not allowed to enter but were taken to a house
of ice. This treatment was devilry.

The old woman told them to go inside and sit down, but the
Listener, who could read her thoughts, told them that if they
sat down they would die. When the door closed upon them, it
became part of the walls, but Haton-dos was not to be outdone.
He sang and his red robin sang and the icehouse began to melt.
The woman brought two kinds of food to kill them. First came
hominy with live leeches in it, blood-sucking creatures that live
on animal blood — a symbol made famous by Dracula and
stories of vampires, and a good symbol for the negative Great
Mother. But the Listener knew how to fool the woman. The
next kettle contained a living flint stone that would cut through
the men who ate it and kill them. Again, Haton-dos won the
contest. About that time, the constant singing of the bird had
melted the house of ice and the men were free.

Each man was assigned a wife and a place in the house of
bark. The youngest and most maleable woman was given to
Haton-dos. The next youngest was given to the next most
powerful and brave of the men after the Listener. His name
translated into English is Hammer-handle-through-his-hip. We
learn later on that the Listener's friend was not only a human
being of power, but also the spirit of winter and frost. When
we hear the frost crackling in the winter it is Hammer-handle-
through-his-hip striking the trees. A human hero, as in the
myths of so many different cultures, can also be a spirit of
nature — an enchanted world indeed. It is difficult to know
whether this man was a hero because of or in spite of the
hammer handle through his hip.

When night came they all went to sleep with their respective wives. One of the most characteristic beliefs of the Seneca, their confidence in the truth of dreams, then betrayed the wicked old woman. In the middle of the night she had a most horrible dream. She got up and rolled around until someone hit her on the head to wake her up. The Listener immediately asked her what she dreamed. Naively she revealed one of her most important secrets. Her dream was that Haton-dos went to the lake and killed the red otter. The Listener reasoned quite correctly that if this was such a horrible thought that he needed to do exactly what the woman feared. His wife was partly in league with him and told him that the red otter was her mother's husband, then went on to tell him that during this venture he must keep the door of the longhouse swinging constantly, or he would die. Haton-dos could meet every challenge. He had stretchable string that he tied to his heel and to the door. As he walked the door kept up its motion, and he stationed his friend Hammer-handle-through-his-hip at the door to be certain that the old woman didn't fasten the door shut.

Unless we pause and look deeply into the symbols of string, thread, and otter we miss the deep archetypal significance of these images. It was the golden thread of Ariadne that saved Theseus from the Minotaur's maze. The Greek Moirai or Fates and the Norse Norns prepared, spun, and cut the thread of human life. Thread is a weaving together of weak fibers to make a strong filament and so implies binding together; it can offer access to the various levels of reality, or it can bind together two human beings and so has sexual implications. For some human beings, rope or string can be a fetish that induces sexual release. We speak of tying the knot of marriage. In this instance, the string protected the Listener's life and kept him in touch with his magic power.

As I first reflected on the image of the otter, it appeared to be merely an ordinary animal found plentifully in the many rivers and lakes of the Iroquois country. I knew that one of the medicine societies that specialized in healing the sick was called the Otter Society. As I looked further I found that in Norse mythology Ottar was a magician (or perhaps minor god) who could take the form of an otter in order to catch salmon. The wicked Loki, who caused so much mischief, killed the otter and had to give his father gold to pay for the murder. Siegried's hunting suit was made of otter skins, and in it he died. In Shakespeare's play *Henry VIII*, a lively discussion occurs as to whether the otter is a fish or animal. Like Ottar, the old woman's husband was a mysterious animal and human and spirit.

As I reflected more and more on the images and symbols of these stories, I was reminded of going through the tomb of Ramses II with the flickering light of a kerosene lamp. On every side I was confronted by the animal-headed gods: jackal-headed Thoth, falcon-headed Osiris. I entered into the dream world. Human bodies (really divine bodies) had heads of bulls, hippos, hawks, rams, snakes. In nearly every culture human beings have seen the divine in the animal-human form. Zeus could assume any animal form to achieve his sometimes questionable ends. The four gospels of Christianity are symbolized by the lion, the bullock, the eagle, and the human being. The Christ is also represented by a fish and by a lamb.

The hero, once again, went east to find the lake of the otter. The Listener could not only listen, he could speak with spiritual power. It may well be that only those who know the secret of deep listening can give forth words of power. Words are produced by breath and are symbolic of either creative or destructive spiritual powers. The ancient semetic hero-god Enlil was the storm, wind, breath, and "creative word" of the god Anu. Christ is the Logos, the creative Word of God.

Haton-dos called to all the denizens of the lake to come forth. They all came forth except the red otter. He then called specifically for this creature. His "word" was so powerful that even the red otter could not resist and appeared. The Listener killed it, dressed it, and chopped the meat into small pieces.

He was about to start home when the magic lake began to rise. In Egyptian hieroglyphics the symbol for lake stands for the mysterious, the unknown. Achilles was bathed in sacred water by his nymph mother, Thetis, who held him by the heels to make him invulnerable. However, the water did not touch his heel and he died when Paris' magic arrow struck him there. Haton-dos fled. Once the water touched his heel and it became raw. Our hero had powers that Achilles did not have. He spit on his hand and rubbed his spittle on his heel and it was healed. The spittle of Jesus restored the blind man. Often spittle represents soul power and is similar in meaning to blood. In some creation stories the creator uses spittle instead of breath and word to endow creation with life.

The Listener came home and prepared a feast of red otter stew. The malicious old woman wanted to get her hands on just one piece of the meat. From this she could have recreated her husband. Haton-dos was wise enough to keep her far from the boiling pot. Then he called the Giant-False-Faces to the feast.

These spirits of the forest accepted the invitation and knocked on the door with mud turtle rattles, which are still used in Seneca ritual. The mud turtle is the foundation of the earth in the original Iroquois creation myth. Then they took two canoe paddles and danced around the kettle, singing. The canoe and paddles were symbolic of the Iroquois way of getting about their lake and river country, again symbols of power. These spirits of the forest then consumed every particle of the stew and were placated. Many of the religious ceremonies reenacted today in the village longhouses in which masked men play the part of the Giant-False-Faces are for the very purpose of pleasing these ambivalent deities. These figures are one of the identifying characteristics of Seneca and Iroquois religion.

After the festivities the men slept soundly, and when they awoke they decided to explore the area in which these women lived. At the foot of the hill they found, to their horror, a Native American Auschwitz: heaps of the bones of the dead who had heeded the old woman's call to look as they came over the mountain. They realized then that they were dealing with the feminine counterpart of the Evil Twin and that she must be destroyed.

They returned to the longhouse and that night the mother had another nightmare. This time she feared that Haton-dos had killed a large bird that was the king of all birds and lived on the top of a large elm tree. The Listener learned from his ambivalent wife that the bird was her mother's oldest son, the primal bird. And just as the witch Gan-nos-gwah turned honest when her death appeared to be near, so the old woman, De-ga-us-ka-u-da-you, now warned the Listener that he must keep the door of the longhouse swinging or he would die. Perhaps she was hoping for mercy.

But why must the door of the mother's longhouse be kept moving and rattling?

The door is another universal symbol. If often appear in dreams. A dark, malicious creature is lurking at the door and trying to force entrance. Frequently, the dreamer is presented with many doors and must decide which to enter. Or, dreamers may find a door within their individual houses, open it, and discover a whole wing of the house they did not know existed. Jesus says: "I am the door." Blood was placed on the doorposts of the Israelites as they celebrated the first passover. The door is an entrance to new possibilities, a way of going from one dimension to another, as the wardrobe doors were in C. S. Lewis' *The Lion, the Witch, and the Wardrobe*. Or, it can signify a protection, a barrier to mystery as in Bluebeard's locked door. I once wrote a book about the resurrection entitled *The Hinge*; that event is our door, which swings upon hinges and gives access to a whole new world. The door of the longhouse must be kept swinging in order to give Haton-dos free access to the territory of the negative Great Mother. She must not hide away, but be kept in the open. This time the Listener simply stationed his mighty frost-king friend at the door to keep it moving.

Haton-dos soon found the tree and commanded it to bend over. He killed the great bird and brought it back to the settlement where he cooked the bird in a large kettle, flesh and feathers. Again the old woman begged for a piece of the flesh or even a feather. With even a fragment of it she could recreate the entire bird. In black witchcraft, a nail paring or a hair or a bit of skin is needed to cast a spell upon an enemy — a piece of the enemy gives access to the victim's life. Again the Giant-False-Faces were called to consume the great bird in an all-night feast of singing and dancing, and then they returned to the forest where they belong.

That night Haton-dos had a horrible dream. He was awakened by De-ga-us-ka-da-you's blow on his head. The old woman asked him what he dreamed. And then, according to traditional Seneca custom, our hero said, "That is for you to find out." The old woman and her daughters had to guess his dream or they would die. All night long they tried, but with no success. He then called the men to come outside and commanded the building to turn to stone with the doors locked to the door frames.

The Listener-shaman took out his red robin and it sang an enchanted song of destruction along with the men. Then, like Joshua at Jericho, they walked round and round the house, singing until it became red hot. The women pleaded to be released, but only the Listener's wife was let out, for she said she had something of great importance to tell him. Soon all the women inside had perished. The old woman's head burst open and an owl came out and flew up through the smoke hole. The others came out as screech owls and foxes and other worthless creatures. In many diverse cultures the owl is related to witches and death. In one Native American story the call of the owl is a signal that death is coming. Lilith, Adam's first wife, was an Owl-goddess. In Egyptian hieroglyphics (image writing) the owl symbolizes night and death. The fox, likewise, is universally used as a symbol to portray a multiplicity of meanings, but most often it is the sly thief, the tricky, unreliable aspect of a person.

And then comes resurrection. How deeply this story touched me when I was a child and knew nothing about the resurrection of Jesus or the vision of Ezekiel of the valley of dry bones coming to life. Indeed, this story prepared me for the deep reality of both accounts. The nine heroes then went to the foot of the hill and gathered all the bones in a heap and put a tepee over the bones. The Listener, the man of power, the shaman, then kicked a tree so that it would fall upon the tepee and called in a loud voice, "Look out for your lives." The bones came to life and fled from the tepee. Among those who rose from the dead was the careless one, their companion who had looked up at the witch. Even the imperfect could be raised from the dead.

One might think that this would end our story, but Haton-dos, like most heroes, had many more trials and adventures to undergo before he achieved his goal. He and his wife again started off to the east and he asked her what important information she still had for him. First she told him about her younger brother who was a young spotted deer. They came to a bog, a swamp, the place of generation, bursting with life. I remember so clearly dreaming of slogging through a swamp, thinking I would never make it through; the person to whom I told the dream saw this as a positive and necessary journey for anyone who wanted to realize his or her potential. The archetypal film, *The Neverending Story*, portrays the potential hero passing through endless and terrifying bogs.

The woman passed through the treacherous bog on solid ground and returned with a fawn, a young deer. The deer is a rich symbol, sacred to Diana. The hind seeking for water is a symbol of the soul searching for God in the Psalms. It is an image of gentleness, grace, timidity, and also of flattery. Did this woman bring the Listener a new aspect of character out of the abundance of the marsh, something he needed for true maturity? Haton-dos placed the spotted fawn on a bark framework that he carried on his back, and they went on together.

The walk to the east continued and his wife then told him of his next danger. His path would take him through a longhouse where he must keep his eyes closed or they would drop out. After receiving this information Haton-dos concluded that his wife could be of no more use to him and that she had been too much in league with her witch mother, been in collusion with her too long. He pushed her over and she dropped dead, turned into a duck, and flew away. This daughter became a useful creature, one of the waterfowl who rescued the Earth Mother. But it is still an ambivalent symbol found in many cultures, a symbol of the love of knowledge, as ducks can dip into the deep, or one of careless freedom, floating along with the tide. The youngest daughter joined her family, but as a more valuable spirit-animal than any of the others. She, at least, had realized that they had behaved wickedly and had warned her mother of the consequences of their actions.

Haton-dos traveled alone with the fawn on his back. Game was plentiful. "He walked the road or path where people always traveled back and forth" — the path we all take from youth to old age, a path that is seldom smooth. Finally he heard singing. The song called him to look at the beautiful women. He remembered to keep his eyes closed; almost through the longhouse, and thinking he was through it, he opened them. The women had a quilt made of deerskins covered with human eyes and his own dropped out upon the buckskin, leaving him blind. The women took away his bow and arrow and the deer. His soul left him. Why had he failed? Was it his pride? Had he thought himself invulnerable? Had he felt himself immune to danger? Was he careless? Or did he need to know despair before he could be a truly whole person, combining gentleness and compassion with his courage and strength? Up to this time his life had been one success after another. Now he was a blind wanderer.

Like Oedipus, he was blind and could only stumble on in despair. Because he was the Listener, he could tell twilight, dawn, and midday by the songs of the birds. He ate the leaves of bushes and drank from the streams. He was nearly naked and he was desperate, but he did not give up. He kept wandering on like the Iroquois hero Hiawatha. Losing sight means losing one's bearings, one's goal. He had reached utter despair, what the alchemists called the *Nigredo* and which they believed was necessary to success in their work. The Listener knew utter hopelessness, yet he kept on.

His rebirth began when he stumbled into a cornfield. He found the ears of corn and ate them. Corn was sacramental to the Native Americans. I am reminded of Jesus and his disciples who wandered through the wheat fields, plucking the grain on the sabbath and eating it. Transformation began in a cornfield — the corn that grew from the Earth Mother's breasts.

The Listener heard someone coming; his early training had kept him alive. The noise he heard was made by a young woman who lived with her mother and worked the cornfield with her. She returned to her mother and told her about the strange creature she had seen. After two encounters with the negative feminine, Haton-dos now meets the positive feminine. Sometimes we need to be blind in order to find life. Blessed are the beggars in spirit, they can find the wholeness of the kingdom. The old woman took him by the hand and said to her daughter, "This disheveled creature is a man." They took him home, washed and fed him, and the old woman said, "We are very fortunate. It seems that he is a brave man." She knew he had been through the house where they take away the eyes of men. What within us robs us of our sight? Is it ever possible to gain true insight until the deep level of the feminine in us appreciates us, sees our bravery, and admires us?

The Listener offered to go out into the cornfield to scare away the crows, but first asked for a bow and arrow. Mother and daughter found an old bow and arrow, then led him out to the edge of the field, near the forest. Waiting here he heard the rattling of leaves. Using his one, smoky arrow, he shot toward the sound. When the women came for him he told them that he had shot something. The women found he had killed a large deer. The women immediately began to dress the deer and Haton-dos cried out, "Let me have the deer's eyes." He put them into his empty sockets and he could see. Now he was able to provide an abundance of game for the three of them. When his substitute eyes grew dim he replaced them with fresh ones from the game he killed. How do we regain our insight, foresight, our ability to see once we have lost it? We need to use whatever partial vision we have until we are given better eyes.

The old woman suggested to her daughter that she should marry this man. When Haton-dos felt at home and comfortable, he took the young girl as his wife.

In about a year, the young woman bore twins. These twins had many of the characteristics of the original twins of the creation myth, but in this case, both twins were good. They carried the strange names of Burnt-belly and Scorched-body, symbols of the fire through which their father had passed. The twins grew very rapidly and soon were young men. Like most of the other characters of the story, the boys had god-like power that was soon evident.

They decided that they would rescue their father's eyes. They went to the house of lost eyes underground and planned a strategy. The younger brother was to become a little duck. When the women came to the spring for water, they would see him and chase him. Then he would enter the womb of one of the women. In a few days he would be born again as a baby. The younger brother was to cry and cry and not stop until they wrapped him in the blanket covered with men's eyes.

Everything worked according to plan. The younger brother cried until he was wrapped in the blanket. He pretended sleep until the women were fast asleep. Then the baby returned to his full size and commanded the women to sleep as if dead. Then he and his brother took the freshest eyes and the bow and arrow with the least dust, as well as the deer on the bark frame. The magic children then set fire to the house of evil and destruction, and it burned until all that remained was ashes.

The boys returned home the underground way, carrying their father's eyes and his possessions. They presented their father with his own eyes, and for the first time he could really see how beautiful his children were. The boys then set out like the original twins — but these twins were going to vanquish everything that was bad and put out of the world everything that destroyed human life.

When the Listener was alone he reflected and remembered his uncle. How could he have forgotten his promise to call upon his uncle in times of need? During all his horrible trials, he had forgotten his uncle-father. As soon as he thought of him, the uncle appeared. How often I find that I forget there are powers that can help me if only I call upon them when I'm in real need. One of the most important lessons I have learned in the last thirty years is this: at the first sign of trouble I need to stop, reflect, and see if I can make it alone, or if I need the power of the spirit that cares for me and will come to my help when I find myself poor in spirit and caught in deep and treacherous water.

Ultimately there is a happy ending, if not in this life, in the beyond. This is the message of this story, for all heroes who keep on the way. In the end they will find the place where, like Haton-dos, his uncle, his wife, his mother-in-law, and the marvelous twins, we can live and grow together in joy. Is there any greater goal to hope for? This deep hope has made the Seneca people the incredible survivors they are. At the deepest level, these people believed that after trial and tribulation, joy, and peace would be theirs.

CHAPTER TWELVE

The Toadstool Eater

A boy and his uncle lived in a log house. The boy was a toadstool eater. His uncle went out hunting every day, but he never brought home any game. His uncle was a good hunter, but he always brought back only mushrooms for the boy. He never brought home animals.

The little boy played with a bow and arrow. He played around the house and became an expert marksman. The boy was growing large. Every time the uncle went away, he leaned a big fallen tree against the door to keep the boy in the house. The boy would look out of the smoke hole where the birds often perched. One day he shot a bird which was on the edge of the smoke hole. He lost his arrow. He wished very much that he could get out. He pulled out a part of the filling between two of the logs which helped make the house. He saw chipmunks, birds, and other game. He longed to hunt them. He made up his mind to go out as soon as his uncle had left the next day.

The next morning the boy was anxious for the time to pass. He looked through the chink in the wall and watched his uncle leave. The boy decided he would watch his uncle come back that day and not go out until the next day. That afternoon he watched for his uncle. He noticed that there was a woman with his uncle when he came back. He saw the woman go away with the game which his uncle had killed. He watched his uncle while he gathered toadstools.

The boy decided to be ready the next day when his uncle went away. The next morning the boy held the door open a little way when his uncle went out, so that it would not close entirely. When his uncle was gone, the boy pushed and pushed on the door until he opened it far enough that he could stand in the doorway. He shot little animals for fun. He left the house. He went on and on.

He came at last to an open space, and he knew at once that someone must live there. A house stood in the middle of the clearing. He went to it and pulled out sticks so that he could see between the logs. He found out what was going on inside the house. The toadstool eater saw a little child tied to a straight board. It seemed like a fat, healthy, happy child. He was anxious to know if the child could use a bow and arrow. He saw on the wall, on the inside of the house, a number of bottles, but he did not know what they were. He gave the child his bow and arrow, and the little boy shot a bottle. They were buckskin bottles, full of bear oil. When the child shot the bottle, the oil squirted all over. The boys thought it was fun, so they kept on shooting the bottles.

At last the toadstool eater grew worried because he had stayed so long. He hurried home. He made things look the same as they had before his uncle went away. His conscience hurt him, but he kept thinking, "I have always been good before." He comforted himself this way.

All at once he saw his uncle coming. His uncle had a bundle on his back. A woman was with him. After his uncle and the woman had talked for a long time, the woman took the bundle. His uncle gathered toadstools. Then he came into the house.

His uncle said, "You have been out doing mischief."

The boy answered, "You shut me in and fastened the door. How could I get out?"

His uncle said, "You have been to that house and you have done a lot of mischief. That woman worked hard to render out the oil and to dry the meat. She is very angry, and she is coming tonight or tomorrow to kill us. She can take the form of a bear. I am going to help you escape. She will kill me anyway, for I cannot escape her wiles."

During the night, the uncle prepared a magic arrow and a bundle. He cut an alder and cleaned out the pith. He made an arrow of it with a head.

He said to the boy, "I am going to make you very small and I will put you and your bundle into this arrow. I have put three things in the bundle: beaver's teeth, a pigeon feather, and a stone which will turn into a rock. I am going to shoot westward with you in the arrow. When the arrow touches the ground, pick up the bundle and run.

"I will tell you what your bundle is good for. When you hear the bear close to you, take the teeth and make a line on the ground. For three days afterward, nothing can cross this line. Three days will give you a good start. Then take the pigeon feather out of your bundle. For three days then you will be a pigeon. You will roost with other pigeons. Throw the magic stone at your enemy. The stone will turn into a large rock. It will crush her."

At daybreak, the boy and his uncle heard the bear coming. They went outside and the bear tried to catch the boy. The boy ran back and forth between the bear's legs. He said, "I am going to fight my uncle's wife. I am going to fight my uncle's wife."

He ran back and forth until he had a chance for a good aim. Then he shot the bear in the white spot in its neck and the bear dropped dead. The uncle took the boy. He shook him. The boy became very small. He put the boy and his bundle inside the arrow. He shot west, and there was a red streak in the air as the arrow flew. When the arrow struck the ground, the boy became full-size. He took the bundle and ran west. He could hear far off the howling of the bear. He knew she had come to life again.

She was still very angry. She did not begin to pursue the boy at once. First she killed the uncle. Then she killed her own child. This was the child the boy had seen in the other house. Then she pursued the boy.

After a while he thought that the bear was close to him. He drew out the beaver teeth that marked a line on the ground. On the other side of the line, between him and the bear, there was suddenly a big swamp. The bear was so angry that she did not notice it and fell in. The boy was frightened. He ran away. He forgot to pick up the beaver's teeth which he had used. But he took the pigeon feather out of his bundle. He turned into a pigeon. He flew up over the swamp and then he flew west. For three nights he roosted like a bird with other pigeons. The third morning when he flew down on the ground, he became a boy again.

In three days the bear got around the swamp to the place where the boy had been. When the three days were up and she followed him, the boy took the stone out of his bundle and threw it. For three days the stone bounded up and down, crushing everything under it. The bear saw that she was in danger, but could not save herself entirely. She had a hind leg crushed by it. For three days she was in pain. In her pain and weakness she had to go slowly. She saw the little magic stone and decided to get it. Now she took the form of a woman. She picked up her crushed leg and carried it on her shoulder. She limped along after the boy.

The boy at last came to a settlement. He had his bow and arrow with him. He saw many boys his own age and size, playing tag. They all looked alike. He didn't tell the boys that he was trying to escape, but he joined in the game. He left his bow and arrow where he could get hold of them quickly. He kept on playing.

All at once the boys saw a woman coming with a broken leg. She carried this broken leg on her shoulder. She was hopping along on one leg. She sat down on the grass. She thought, "Why, you are fine looking boys, but you all look alike." While the toadstool eater was playing, he ran near the woman. The second time he ran near her again. This time he snatched her broken leg and threw it away. He said, "Broken leg, you must fly away over the seas. Broken leg, you must fly away over the seas." Her leg flew out of sight. She begged the boys not to kill her.

Then the boys knew she was a witch and they decided to pull her arms out. So they pulled her arms out and threw them away. Then they tore her all to pieces and threw her in all directions. After they had done that, they went back to their play, and they are probably playing there yet.

CHAPTER THIRTEEN

Mischief, Evil, and Redemption

The theme of magic and witchcraft runs through all of these legends. Most of the stories are very serious. Evil and destructiveness must be eliminated and this is the hero's serious task. However, in this story we find a playfulness, a childlike quality we do not find in the others. We find many of the same symbols and some fascinating new ones, but throughout this tale there is a lighter touch. We begin with the protective, bewitched uncle-father who knew how dangerous the outside world could be. Indeed, he was married to a witch and kept her supplied with all the best game the forest could provide. His nephew, however, was fed only mushrooms and toadstools and never was allowed out of the house.

As the child grew older, he played with a bow and arrow until he became an expert marksman. One day he shot a bird sitting on the smoke hole of their log cabin. He lost his arrow and wondered how he could get out to retrieve it. He became curious about the world outside. His first mischief was to dig out some of the mud and sticks used to chink up the space between the logs and keep their cabin comfortable. Outside he saw chipmunks and squirrels, woodchucks, and all sorts of birds. Like most playful children, he longed to go out and use his hunting skill. We can be quite sure that he filled up the hole he made before his protector returned.

We find few suggestions that mushrooms or toadstools were a significant element in the diet of the Iroquois. They were undoubtedly eaten in times of famine and the herbalists would have known their medicinal and hallucinogenic properties. Dionysus was a toadstool god before he came a wine god. This child was certainly given a shaman's diet. A people who valued dreams and visions as greatly as the Seneca would have heard echoes in this story that would have escaped most Western ears before Carlos Castanada's stories about Don Juan. Mushrooms are also connected with fairies; they grow up overnight as if by magic. Mushrooms can also signify poison and death, but their main significance in this story is their connection with the earth-spirits, mystery, and magical power.

This trickster hero then made his plans very carefully. Instead of immediately escaping his prison, he watched his uncle go and return. To the boy's surprise he returned with a woman to whom he gave all his fine game — bear and elk and deer — and only then did he pick the mushroom-toadstool food for his nephew. This boy was very careful and astute. When the uncle tried to close the door securely with a big log as he left the next day, his nephew pushed against it and kept it slightly ajar; at last he was able to get out. Once out he shot all sorts of little animals just for the fun of it. Then he wandered out into the forest until he found an open space and another log cabin. He pulled out some twigs between the logs and peeked in. He saw a child on a cradle board.

He entered the cabin, found this child could use a bow and arrow, and together they shot arrows into buckskin bottles of bear oil; the oil squirted out in all directions much to their delight. Precious bear oil made mud of the cabin floor. I will never forget having fun at age five or six by mixing all the different chemicals in my older brother's chemistry set, which earned me the rage of my father. My work had made a delightful mess. The story suggests a different attitude on the part of the Iroquois toward children than one finds in urbanized Western society.

How totally characteristic this child was when he was accused of creating havoc. He simply denied it and he was not punished, even though it would mean the death of the uncle and the child. Instead of discipline, the magical uncle gave the boy a medicine bundle consisting of a beaver's tooth, a pigeon's feather, and a small stone. During the night he made a magic arrow out of a pith-filled alder branch. He cleaned out the pith to make a hiding place for the boy. He intended to speed the boy and his bundle far to the west when the witch-woman transformed herself into a fierce bear, the most dangerous animal known to the Iroquois, and came crashing through the forest seeking her revenge.

Four symbolic gifts were given to the boy, gifts that come from the very depth of the collective unconscious. To people who lived by the use of the arrow and the bow, the arrow was life-giving. The arrow, like the hand, is used to indicate direction to a goal. Often arrows were used in divining, with words written upon them. The arrow was seen as a sign of deliverance among the Hebrews and also as a symbol of death; the arrow that flies by day is seen as equivalent to the pestilence that destroys by night. Cupid (Eros) creates the madness of love with his arrow. But this is a hollow arrow in which the uncle was to send the boy on the first stage of his magic flight.

The uncle also had the power to make the youth and his bundle small enough to fit into the space the pith had occupied. Alice, as she ate a mushroom, grew smaller and larger in Lewis Carroll's wonderland. It is only a step from being small enough to fit into a hollow arrow to becoming invisible. In several recent adventure movies, human beings shrink to tiny size.

In the spiritual world and in the collective unconscious, space is entirely relative. In the real physical world, infinitely tiny electrons spin around the nucleus of the atom as planets spin around the sun. This truly is a magical world in which we live.

The beaver's teeth are huge, enabling the beaver to cut down large trees to build the dams in which it lives. Before human beings began producing axes and saws in the Iron Age, they could not match the beaver's skill or diligence. We still use the expression "busy as a beaver." These huge teeth are symbols of mana and power. With the teeth, our hero could draw a line in the dirt and for three days nothing would be able to follow him.

The pigeon feather is a symbol of the ability to fly like a bird. In this myth it enabled the boy to become a pigeon and so hide from his enemy. We earthbound creatures (until very recently) saw the feather as a symbol of flight, lightness, spirituality. In the Egyptian myth, the human soul will be weighed against a feather to see if it is pure.

The small stone recalls the story of David and Goliath, the stone as an instrument of destruction, the stone hurled by the catapult, the avalanche of boulders used by ambushers to destroy the enemy. This, however, is a magic stone that knows no spacial limits and, when hurled at its foe, will pursue its victim until it hits its mark.

The witch-bear appeared and was shot dead, but evil is seldom destroyed by one arrow. However, its temporary death gave the uncle time to shake the boy and his bundle down to size, to put them into the arrow, and to shoot them to the west, toward the sunset, darkness and transformation, the night sea journey.

The witch-bear came back to life, now more ferocious than before. She was furious about the destruction of her carefully rendered bear oil and now she was angry about being kept from her revenge. Before starting on her pursuit of the boy, like Medea, she killed her own child and the uncle-husband. Then she went on her way.

As I listen to these legends again and again, I find deeper and deeper levels of meaning. In the first three or four readings I missed the significance of the uncle-protector. He had tried to save his nephew from confronting the evil to which he was married, the malicious evil to which the boy was related. Once he realized that the boy now must face the dark side of reality, the uncle became a savior-figure. He did not use his magic powers to save himself, but lay down his life so that his playful, mischievous charge might be saved. He and the baby died in order that the hero might live. The ancient theme of the savior who dies so others may live, lies in the heart of this story. This image of one who dies for another is one of the most powerful symbols of mythology. This was the essence of the Christian message that gave hope to a disintegrating ancient world. Dickens' *A Tale of Two Cities* and Hugo's novel *Les Misérables* touch the deepest level of the human heart and psyche.

The bear's chase began. She was stopped by the power of the beaver's tooth and the pigeon feather. Her nemesis, however, was the little stone that the hero hurled at his pursuer. It grew into a huge boulder, which followed the witch-bear like the smart bombs over Baghdad. It finally struck its mark and crushed one of the bear's legs. The witch resumed her human form and we are given the humorous image of the witch carrying her crushed leg over her shoulder, still hopping along, hoping to find and destroy her enemy. Her single-minded vengeance brought her annihilation.

She finally found the boy in a settlement playing with other children. The hero snatched her leg from her and hurled it far, far away. Then all the boys fell upon the witch and tore her to pieces, as the women Bacchantes of ancient Greece tore apart those who intruded upon their ecstatic and wild religious rites. And then the boys went back to their play. The playful, childlike trickster destroyed the witch. Sometimes this same part of us can still destroy the evil that could do us in. This tale of magic and enchantment springs out of the mysterious depth of the human soul. We need to be childlike and playful if we wish to stay in touch with this enchanted world of universal images. Jesus said to his disciples, "except you become as little children, you cannot enter the kingdom of heaven."

We also need a savior figure who gives us the wisdom and the power to find our way in an often treacherous world. We need to find that self-giving and creative aspect of reality that is willing to die for us even in our childish mischief and unconsciousness. This forgiving and enlightening reality selected a drunken, broken down old warrior at the point of death and spoke to Handsome Lake. The prophet was reborn and so were his dispirited people. The uncle-protector is a symbol of this spiritual reality which Christians see incarnate in Jesus of Nazareth.[1]

CHAPTER FOURTEEN

The Beautiful Head

An uncle and his nephew lived in a house by themselves. Ever since the boy had been old enough to wield the bow and arrow, he had been learning to shoot straight. He practiced with the bow and arrow as he played around the house. He had a wild animal's foot to shoot at as a target.

As soon as the boy was old enough to leave the house, his uncle said, "You might as well begin shooting now. Anything you meet you are to shoot, cut off its head, and bring the head home."

After a while the boy went into the woods. He shot woodchucks and squirrels. He brought home their heads. His uncle told the boy the names of the animals whose heads he brought home.

Years passed by. He brought home all kinds of heads, from the smallest animals as well as the largest. All that time he killed different kinds of animals and learned their names. He went farther and farther into the woods.

One day, when he was still a young man, he went farther than he had ever gone. He heard the noise of a great gathering of people who were hooting and calling. He went in the direction of the noise and came to an open field. In the center of it stood a tree. In the tree he saw a strange animal. The tree had two limbs branching out at the same height but in opposite directions. The young man noticed that the animal in the tree had the features of a human being and had beautiful hair, red and fine as corn silk. He watched the animal in the tree and the people who filled the field. All the people were trying to kill the human-like animal. Every time an arrow was shot at the animal, the animal jumped to the opposite branch. The young man walked away.

He went through the woods, crept through a hollow fallen tree, and came out as an old man. He was bent and he was coughing. When he had disguised himself in this way so that no one would know who he was, he went back to the people. They wished someone would kill the animal. The old man walked slowly about. He looked at the people and he looked at the tree.

The young men said to him, "Go away! You can't hit it."

They tried to push him away. He kept getting nearer the tree.

They said to him, "That is a poor-looking bow, and your arrow is crooked. Throw those worthless sticks away!"

He paid no attention, but kept getting nearer the tree. He pointed his arrow at the animal.

The people said to him, "You need not try to shoot. Your arrow can't touch the animal."

He said, "You keep back out of my way. I am going to try."

He thought what he should do. He decided to shoot at the branch where the animal was not. He shot at the empty limb. When he shot, the animal jumped to the empty limb just in time to be hit by the arrow. The arrow killed the animal instantly, and it fell to the ground. He hurried to the fallen tree to get his knife which he had left there. He cut off the head of the animal. Then he went through the log to be changed into a young man again. He ran towards home. The people followed him, but no one overtook him. They did not know who he was.

When he reached home, the boy said to his uncle, "I have a new head to show you." He showed his uncle the head with the fine red hair.

His uncle said, "That is the head you have been hunting for ever since you were a little boy."

All the animals of the woods followed the head to the young man's home. The old man put the head away in a bark barrel and covered it with deerskin. He placed it in a bark dish before he put it in the bark barrel. The next morning all the animals were flocking about the door, in the trees, and on the housetop.

There were birds and beasts. The young man said to the animals, "Keep away! Keep back! We won't hurt you." The young man and his uncle had plenty of game. They killed all kinds of animals — bears, deer, elks — all the kinds of game they could eat.

It was not long before some people came. They said, "We would like to see the beautiful head you have."

The uncle got out little birds' heads. The people were very particular. They said, "No, we want to see the head with red hair, the head of the strange animal you killed."

They kept asking him and urging him, but he would not let them see the beautiful head. They went away. Every day different people came to see the head. They offered to pay, but the old man said, "No, I have nothing but these little heads."

Time passed by. One night two women came, traveling in a canoe. They came to the roof of the house and climbed down through the chimney to the bark barrel. They stole the head. As they were going back up the chimney, the young man shot one of the women in her back. When they were outside, they climbed into their canoe. They paddled in the air as if they were in the water. The young man started after them. He overtook the boat and held it by the end and kept his feet on the ground.

When the women saw him, they said, "You let go or we will kill you." They showed their weapons. He let go of the boat and the women went on.

The young man followed them and bothered them so that they could not go fast. Finally he went back home. He told his uncle that he was going after the head and that he would surely get it.

He went in the direction the women had gone. It took him a long time to reach the village where they lived. He found a great many people there. Before he entered the village, he crept into a hollow fallen tree and came out disguised as an old man. Then he went to the gathering of the people. They told him that the daughter of the chief was very sick. Two of his daughters had been away in search of something. One sister was very sick with an arrow in her back. The chief had offered her to any man who would pull out the arrow. It had stuck fast in her flesh. No one could pull it out. All the young men had tried.

Finally the young man who was in search of the beautiful head said to the chief, "I am going to try to pull out the arrow. I am old. I don't want the woman, but I will relieve her suffering."

The Chief told him he might try. The young man who was disguised as an old man sang, "I came here to make peace, to relieve the sick woman. .I came here to make peace, to relieve the sick woman. I came here to make peace, to relieve the sick woman."

He walked towards the bed where the girl was lying on her face. As he sang, the arrow started to come out without being touched. When it was nearly out, a young man who was standing nearby snatched the arrow. But instead of coming out it went farther into the girl's back. It went out of sight in the flesh. The old man who was singing stopped and scolded the young man. The chief ordered the young man who had tried to get the arrow tied up and carried off. He had him guarded so that he could not come back. The young man who appeared as an old man started to go away.

The chief said, "No, you must not go. You sing again because the arrow minds you. The arrow started to come out."

Before he began singing this time, the old man went away for a short time. He promised to come back. Just outside the village, in the woods, stood the house of a widow woman. When he left the sick girl, he went to this house. He had something to eat. Then he went into his hollow fallen tree and called for many rats to get together.

The rats came and he said to them, "You dig underground from the place where the head is to this tree so that the head will roll this way."

The rats got in line, ready to work. He told them where the head was hidden in the barrel. In the night they dug and dug. He didn't dare leave until he was sure they would have success. He waited for his workers, whom he had promised to pay. He decided to go and see the sick woman in the morning.

At daylight he went to the hollow fallen tree and called to the rats, "How are you getting along? How far are you?"

They answered, "We are here at the tree." They gave him the head that they had brought underground. He took the head and shook it. It grew small enough so that he could put it in a bag he carried.

Then he went back to the sick woman. He began to sing, "I came here to make peace, to relieve the sick woman. I came here to make peace, to relieve the sick woman. I came here to make peace, to relieve the sick woman."

He circled around and around the bed. The arrow came out. The guards kept watch so that no one should try to take it. The singer picked up the arrow and left.

The people called, "Stop! Stop! You may have the woman for your wife."

He said, "No, I am an old man. I am not fit to take care of a woman."

Then he went back to the widow's home. He said to her, "I am going to destroy the village, but I will make an exception of you. You were good to me, so I will save you. You watch the fire, and after the village is burned, you follow me to my home. If you follow a red line which you will see in the sky, you will reach my home safely."

The young man had a red iron ring around his neck. He took off this ring and threw it over the settlement. It started a fire which burned in a circle all around the village. After the widow had set out, he went to the hollow fallen tree and took out the head and the bow and arrow he had left there. Then he went back to his uncle.

His uncle had been wishing that the boy would come back and bring the head. When he saw the boy coming, he went to meet him. He ran because he was in such a hurry to know if the beautiful head was safe. He stumbled and fell as he ran. The boy said to his uncle, "You were careless. Now you must hide the head where it cannot be stolen."

The old man put the head under his bed. In a few days the animals came back to the dooryard and the tree and the house-top. They had gone away when the head was stolen.

In a number of days the widow came. She said that the village was burned up. The widow had five children, two girls and three boys. They made their home with the young man and his uncle. They are living there yet, and they have plenty of game to eat.

CHAPTER FIFTEEN

The Deep Mystery and Power of the Human Soul

The task of the uncle-father was to teach and train the boy in his charge to deal with the hostile environment in which the Iroquois lived. He shared all the skills needed to survive in the wilderness. Girls were more likely to be reared in a village where they learned how to cultivate the corn and squash and beans and make buckskin clothes. In addition to learning these outer skills, they were taught the equally important wisdom about the spiritual world. They learned how to participate in the rituals of their people, as we described earlier. When the teachers were men or women of power, they shared the methods of using spiritual power with those who were wise enough to use them.

The unnamed youth in this myth was very young when a bow and arrow were placed in his hands and he learned to be a marksman. His first target was an animal's foot on the other side of their log home. When I was a child living in rural Pennsylvania, many people carried rabbits' feet in their pockets as good luck charms. The foot is the symbol of our contact with the earth, the mother, reality. The symbol of the foot has dozens of other meanings, but what a wonderful target for the growing sharpshooter. And he was learning to shoot at more than he knew. When the boy was old enough to venture into the forest alone, he shot first small animals and then larger game. He brought home the severed heads and his uncle told him the names and habits of the creatures he had slain. We will see a deeper significance in the head symbol shortly.

One day our skilled hunter went further away from home than he had ever been before. He heard the hooting and hubbub of many excited people. In an open field he saw a tree in the form of a cross with two limbs branching out opposite each other. On one branch was the strangest creature he had ever seen. The beast had a human head with beautiful hair, red and fine as corn silk. A great number of people were trying to shoot this strange and beautiful sphinx-like being. The human-animal was too quick for any of the expert hunters, jumping from one branch to another. The young hero knew that he *must* have this head, but his ordinary skill would not suffice.

Before we go further, let us look at the archetypal symbols that poured out in a few lines. The cross-like tree is a very special place. Long before the cross became the Christian symbol for overcoming evil and death, the intersecting lines of the cross had fascinated humankind. We find these lines in ancient rock carvings and in pottery designs. When the cross was found naturally occurring in a stone or a tree, it had special significance. The cross speaks of the mystery of life; combined with the tree, the depth of the symbol is compounded. According to Seneca myth the earth was created by the tree of life falling through a hole in the sky into the great and fertile dark water. The cross has four points and is related to the number four, the quaternity. One of the most important symbols of the Tarot cards is the hanged man, who is usually depicted as hanging upside down from a tree. Woden (Odin) hung nine nights on Yggdrasil, the world-tree of Norse myth, in order to obtain the runes. The cross symbol can signify life, creation, death, initiation, protection, heaven, the sign that illiterate people use to indicate their names, the mandala. The Chi-Rho Cross came to Constantine in a vision and signified victory to him; to the early Church it represented freedom from persecution. The hero has come to the center, to the heart of being, to the place of transformation.

His task was to take possession of the beautiful head with the exquisite and radiant red hair. Except when I am looking for meaning in my dreams, I seldom stop to listen to the symbols that I use or that come to me in myth and imagination. In Ad de Vries' *Dictionary of Symbols and Imagery* (the most comprehensive and sophisticated lexicon of symbols I know) two entire pages are devoted to the symbolic meaning of hair, another page to the head as an image signifying many different ideas, a whole column to the human-headed animal, and another column to Oedipus who answered the riddle of the human-headed lion. I find myself almost overwhelmed by the symbols that bubble out of our depth. A most important insight came to me in analysis when in midlife I dreamed of being in a boarding house in Phoenix where I had lived as a youth. I saw a boar's head wink at me from the plate rail that ran around the dining room. In the place of rebirth, Phoenix, I saw the animal that killed Adonis. I needed to be aware and to beware of the wild boar, the negative side of the great mother Venus that slew Adonis after he had made love to her. Again, in talking to a dream turtle in imagination I was led for many hundreds of pages through the symbolic depth within and beyond myself.

The strange animal that is partly human is an archetypal figure representing the union of our intellectual, thinking, human side with our animal, instinctual nature, a symbol of wholeness. While wandering through the Louvre once, I came upon a recumbent statue facing the wall and a worn pathway leading behind the marble figure. I found an hermaphrodite with breasts and male genitals. In a less prudish age, this was another symbol of wholeness.

How do we capture this animal with a handsome human head and silk-like red hair? The head is an image pregnant with significance: human intellect and wisdom, spiritual life. The severed head of the hero was buried at strategic points to guard against enemy attack. Often in mythology and dreams severed heads talk, as my boar's head winked at me. The head is the central control house of the person. It also can signify masculinity, virility, fertility (Athena burst forth from Zeus' head). In alchemy the head is the vessel of transformation, power, and even of the Universe itself. In Hegel's discussion of the symbols used in art, he saw the sphinx as the perfect symbol of the symbolic itself.

The hair as a symbol again simply explodes with connections and allusion and contents. In some myths red hair points to the devil, or the hair of the god of the underworld, Set or Radamanthus, and so children with red hair needed special charms to protect them. Red hair often signifies a fiery temperament; I once dreamed of a difficult blond stepmother as having red hair. Red hair was very unusual among the Native Americans. For them it probably related to mystery, magical power, and energy. Sampson's superhuman strength left him when Delilah cut off his hair. Women were once required to cover their heads in church and in public because the angels were supposedly so attracted to women's hair that they were seduced by it. Prostitutes proclaimed their profession in Corinth by letting their long hair hang down unveiled around their shoulders. The woman who wiped Jesus' feet with her loose hair gave evidence of her background; chaste Hebrew women wore braided hair and veils.

I was writing and reading about this section on board ship and was struck by the fact that sailors in several cultures felt that cutting hair or paring fingernails could bring bad luck. On a calm sea the trimming of either might even raise a storm.

The young man in our story wanted this head, this strange symbol of power and wholeness. He knew, however, that he could not obtain it by ordinary means. He needed to rely upon magic and trickery. He went through the woods until he discovered the symbolic fallen hollow tree. He entered the womb of the tree and emerged reborn as he wished to be, as an old and decrepit man, with a crooked bow and a crooked arrow. He became the fool. The other hunters made fun of him. He had deceived them and he also deceived the magical animal on the tree-cross. Then he added wisdom and cleverness to magic. Jesus said that we need to be as gentle as doves and as wise as serpents. Many religious people forget this truth and get nowhere on the spiritual journey.

The hero paid no attention to the mockery of the young men milling around the tree. Instead of aiming directly at the sphinx-like creature, he aimed at the place to which the beast jumped and he killed it with his crooked arrow. Carrying his prize, he hurried to the fallen tree where he had left his knife, and cut off its head. Then he passed through the tree womb and became himself again and ran home to show his uncle his trophy. The uncle then revealed his magical wisdom by saying to him, "This is the head you have been hunting for ever since you were a boy." The young man had achieved the first level of his individuation. The uncle had been training the boy to achieve this very goal.

The uncle preserved the head by placing it in a bark dish, in a bark barrel, and covering it with deerskin. Why bark? At the same time that lumbermen were logging the great redwoods of California, they were also cutting down the tanoaks. These trees were stripped of bark and the bark was used in the tanning of leather. This realistic touch shows how well the Native Americans knew the values of the herbs and trees among which they lived. Once the head was safely preserved and hidden away, the animals of the forest came flocking around the house where the magical head was kept. The youth and his uncle even had to tell the bears, deer, and elks to go away. From that time on they never lacked for game. It was not long before a steady stream of people came asking to see the beautiful head; some were even willing to pay to see it, but the head was never shown.

Beware of women who come through the sky paddling their canoe in the air! According to the Iroquois, witches had this kind of power and they could also cast spells at a great distance. One night two women came in their airborne canoe in search of the beautiful head. In the Greek myth of Oedipus, the Sphinx was a feminine creature with the head, breasts, and arms of a woman and the body of a lioness, a perfect image of the negative Great Mother, feared both by the Greeks and the Iroquois. Jung has suggested that Oedipus should have had more awe and fear of this creature who had been sent by the great Greek Mother Goddess, Hera, to trick the arrogant hero. Had he possessed a more reasonable fear of the mystery and holiness of the feminine, he might have avoided killing his father and marrying his mother and the disaster that followed. I can hardly imagine the Iroquois considering a man's head with silky red hair as beautiful. These women and this head are both symbols and images of the great Mother Goddess from whose dominance the Iroquois had only recently been liberated. One does not conquer the Mother Goddess with the flight of just one magic arrow. The bear in the previous story came back to life. In this story the women-witches-goddesses came in their canoe, slipped down through the chimney hole, stole the head, and then started to leave the way they came. The young hero shot one of the women in the back and then pursued them as they left in their canoe.

He soon discovered that he could not stop them by his own power. He returned to tell his uncle that he would find and bring back the head. He started in the direction the women had fled. At last he came to a large village where the women lived. Again he passed through the womb of wood, the hollow tree, and came out as an old man. He mingled with the people and discovered that the women were daughters of the chief and one was very sick with an arrow through her back. Anyone who could pull the arrow from the young woman could have her for his wife; none had been successful. The youth, disguised as an old man, sang a song and the arrow began to emerge. When a youth standing nearby tried to snatch it out, the arrow burrowed deeper into her back.

Before our hero was willing to try the healing song again, he left the chief's home. The young-old man found a widow woman with five children who was kind to him, invited him in, gave him food to eat, and allowed him to rest. I am reminded of the widows who were kind to the Hebrew prophets, Elijah and Elisha. The hero needed to be in touch with the positive side of the feminine nature if he were to be whole and successful in his quest. Then he went back to his hollow log with a plan. He now knew where the head was hidden. By magic he called together a great company of rats and told them to dig through the ground, come up where the head was kept, and bring it back.

Rats and mice have received a very bad press as carriers of disease. Mice and rats cause irrational fear in many people. Yet in myth and folklore they have many positive connotations. In dreams they often represent our instincts, our animal instinctive power that can be either creative or destructive. In Celtic myths the rat is related to the god Cerunnus and has positive earthy associations. If all the rats leave a ship it is doomed, and the word "rat" has been taboo at sea.

In Aesop's fable 94, the mouse outwitted the cat. Mice are also symbols of humility and lack of arrogance. The hero knows how to call upon the humble, chthonic, gnome-like powers as well as heavenly ones. The rats willingly obliged the hero and the old-young man waited as they burrow through the night. In the morning the rats presented the hero with the head and were paid for their labor. When we use our instinctual power we need to acknowledge it and reward it. He then shook the head to make it small enough to fit into his pouch.

Still disguised as an old man, he returned to the house of the sick woman. He repeated his chant as he circled around and around the bed, a strange chant for one who is about to destroy the whole village, "I came here to make peace, to relieve the sick woman." The arrow came out and he left. He returned to the widow's house and warned her that he was going to destroy the whole village, but she and her children were to leave the town and follow him.

The next episode of the myth is reminiscent of Jahweh and the wicked cities of Sodom and Gomorrah. Around his neck the youth wore a red, iron ring, a union of three incredibly powerful symbols. Iron is metal of which witches are afraid and has scores of meanings. However, the Iroquois knew little of iron before the coming of the Europeans. I wonder if the ring might have been a copper or gold ring that might have made its way north from Mexican civilization or from the Creek Native Americans in Georgia who used copper for ornaments. This was a fiery ring and one that could set fire to a whole village. The hero has a Zeus-like aspect; he appears more godlike than human.

The mysteries of the circle of Stonehenge, of wedding rings, of mandalas, of magic circles come to mind as we look at the symbol of the ring. The fine modern myth of Tolkien revolves around a ring of power. This collar of fiery power burned up the city after this man of power had thrown it over the settlement. Making sure that the widow and her family were on their way, he went back to the hollow log where he had left his bow and arrow and the beautiful head.

The hero then went back to his uncle's home. His uncle stumbled as he ran to greet the victorious youth. The latter now took charge and told the uncle to be more careful in hiding the head. In a few days the widow arrived with her children, and the eight of them, another number of totality, lived on happily with all the game that they could use. The beautiful head was infallible hunting-medicine. Von Franz has suggested that the number of characters at the beginning and end of a folktale are important. We began with two men and ended with five males and three females. We again have the number symbolic of wholeness.

CHAPTER SIXTEEN

The Young Man's Revenge

There was a long war between two peoples who spoke different tongues. When the war ended, the victors started on their way home. They carried with them the spoils they took and their prisoners. At the close of the day, two prisoners, a mother and her little boy, lay down to sleep. The boy slept well, but the mother's rest was broken.

In the morning the mother said to the boy, "Last night I dreamed that I am going to be killed. You are to be saved. Be brave, my son, and revenge your mother's death." He promised that he would remember her and someday take revenge.

That day the victors decided that the woman would be of no use to them. They killed her. When she was dead and the boy was left alone, they took the boy with them.

Soon the march was at an end. When they reached the settlement, the warriors were received with great rejoicing. The boy watched everything. A great feast was prepared. Around the fire stood a crowd of men. In one place there was an opening and two rows of men stood facing each other. The rows of men reached to the longhouse where inside the door, on the floor, was a cougar's skin.

The boy was told that he must run the gauntlet. He was forced to walk over the fire, which had died down to a bed of coals. The warriors told him to dance on the coals. While they sang their songs, he danced until his feet were blistered. He was young and he wished he could die. But he remembered his promise to his mother to avenge her death, and that he must live until he could have revenge. He danced until the blisters on his feet broke.

Then the men called, "Run through the gauntlet and try to reach the cougar's skin!" The boy ran. Each man hit him with a stick as he ran past. But he was not overcome. He reached the cougar's skin and fell exhausted upon it.

There was a cry, "He is a brave boy! He is a brave boy! We will let him live."

Among the people were a man and his wife whose son had died. They said, "We will adopt this brave boy and make him our son. He is young and he will forget his own home and his own people." They took the boy home and put bear oil over his back and wrapped him in soft skin. Each day they loved him more. As he grew to be a young man, he never said anything about his mother, but he did not forget his promise to her.

Each year the young men of the settlement went to the woods to get maple sugar. They spent several weeks away from home. The captive boy wished to go, but they would not take him. He did all he could to win their trust. At last, one year they made him a member of the council. They left him in charge of the settlement while they were gone. He judged justly and well.

When the men returned from the sugar camp, they said, "Next year, you may go with us."

He said, "I know a very good place for a camp, and I will lead you to it."

The next spring came. The men started for the sugar camp. The captive boy said good-bye to his uncle. He knew he would never see him again. The captive boy led the men. When they had gone a long distance, he stopped and gave directions.

He said to two of the men, "You go towards the east and circle about until you come to that tall tree on yonder mountain."

To two other men he said, "You go towards the west and at last reach that tall tree on yonder mountain."

He separated all of the men into groups of two and had each two take a different trail which was to lead to that tall tree on yonder mountain. He took two men with him. As soon as the others were out of sight and hearing, he killed the two men who were with him. Then he hurried around the foot of that yonder mountain.

There was a settlement there. He saw an old woman in the woods, digging roots. He whispered in her ear. She hastened to the settlement. He went here and there about the outskirts of the village. To each man, woman, and child he saw, he whispered. They all hurried to the village. Soon a large band of warriors met him outside the settlement. They went with him to that tall tree on the mountaintop. Soon the two men who had taken the eastern route came. The warriors killed them. Then the two men who had gone west reached the mountaintop. The warriors killed them, too. As each pair came, they were killed, until all who had left for the sugar camp were dead.

The young man had remembered his promise to his mother. He had his revenge. The warriors who had helped him were his own people. He returned with them to the valley and became their chief.

A VERY HUMAN TALE

In this tale we leave the world of the superhuman, the mysterious, and return to the ordinary world of Iroquois life. Constant warfare continued to plague the relations of many Native American tribes. Warfare was more of a game with high stakes than a desire to exterminate and destroy. The same view of war existed among the tribes of southern Africa until the Zulu chief Shakti turned war into the serious business of conquering and assimilating tribe after tribe.

The setting for this tale had occurred again and again. A neighboring group of Native Americans went on the warpath and started war with another people. The victors took with them the spoils of war and their prisoners. We have seen already some of what prisoners had to endure. Prisoners not worth keeping were slain. For this reason the Iroquois federation of the equal nations was a tremendous step toward peace and civilization.

Among the prisoners taken on one occasion were a boy and his mother. The boy did not realize what lay in store for him and slept well. His mother, however, was a true Seneca; she dreamed that she was going to be killed, but the boy would survive. She asked him to revenge his mother's death. The boy promised. The mother's dream was precognitive. Such dreams of the future are recorded among all human cultures. Since an old woman would be of no use to them, the captors killed her and took the boy with them.

The Iroquois valued bravery, courage, and endurance of pain above all other virtues for men and boys. The captured youth was forced to dance through smoldering coals, and then to run the gauntlet. He fell exhausted, but without a cry of pain or a tear, upon the cougar skin that was placed at the end of the ordeal.

The youth had made it and was adopted Iroquois-style into a family of that nation. The foster parents cared for the boy greatly and thought that he would forget his own tribe and family. Little did they know of the promise that he had made to his mother or his resolve to keep it. His model behavior convinced his parents and the tribe that he was fully integrated, but the young man was plotting his escape and his revenge.

One of the great Iroquois festivals is the spring festival that occurred as the sweet sap of maple trees began to flow. The trees were tapped, the sap collected and boiled down into syrup and sugar. The captive was as clever and wise as he was brave. When the sugaring time approached, he told the leaders that he had found a fine stand of maples to which he would lead them. The boy said good-bye to his uncle (the generic name for father or male protector) and set off with the men for the sugar camp.

The whole group followed the young man's leadership. He separated the group into pairs and sent them in different directions. He selected two companions to go with him to meet at a tall tree on yonder mountain. Soon after they were on their way, the young man killed his two companions.

Not only had he been a model member of the tribe that had adopted him, he had been planning and scouting out the countryside. He had found the way back to his own people. Once he was alone he hurried to his own people. He told them what he had planned and soon a large band of warriors were gathered in the village. They set out with him to the mountain.

As the people came to the sugar camp, two by two, carrying their bark buckets for maple sap, the warriors easily killed all of those who had set out with him.

This story might be a remembrance of the time before Hiawatha when the various nations of Iroquois had been destroying one another. The moral of this story is very clear. Promises of vengeance and courage are goals that cannot be forgotten among warring people. The young man became chief of his own village and its hero. His mother's death was avenged. The desire for revenge or avenging a wrong are not unknown in the depth of most of us. Betrayal and injury are forgotten only with divine help. It was true for the Iroquois and is still true for most of us.

CHAPTER SEVENTEEN

The Man-Eater

A young man lived alone with his uncle. The uncle kept the young man in the house, under the bed. The boy was fed under the bed and stayed there all the time. The bed was made from trees. The roots grew over the body of the boy to keep him from running away. His uncle told him what happened outside of the house.

One spring day, the uncle went out to plant corn. While he was planting, he heard a song. The song said that the young man was going to get out. His uncle ran towards the house. As he ran, he spilled all of the corn he had not yet planted. He went into the house and looked under the bed. He found that the boy had his shoulders free and was trying to get out. The old man pushed the young man back under the roots and bound him down. He advised the young man to stay in. The boy promised to stay in. The uncle was afraid that the boy would get away, and so he stayed with the boy for a long time.

The boy did not try to free himself. So one day the uncle went away to get slippery elm bark to make ropes. While he was working, he again heard a song. Again the song said that the boy was getting out from under the bed. The uncle ran back home. On the way he dropped his bark and kept slipping on it and falling. When he got to the house and looked under the bed, he found that the boy was free as far as his waist.

The uncle felt very bad. He said, "I am afraid that you will get killed. You are the only one of your tribe left. All the rest were killed by a man-eater on an island nearby."

Years afterward, the boy got up without his uncle being warned by a song. He thought of the island where there was a man-eater and decided that he would kill the man-eater. He said to his uncle that he was going. His uncle told him that he must not go, but he disobeyed his uncle. He had not walked far when he came to a little stream of water which separated him from the island. He crossed the stream and walked around the island.

When he wanted to go back home, he could not find the stream. It had grown very, very wide. This island was now in the midst of a sea. He sat down and moaned and then walked around the island again. This time he came across something covered by sand. He looked carefully and saw that it was the upper half of a skeleton.

The skeleton whispered to him, "I am your brother. The man-eater who owns this island will be here at bedtime with his dogs. He and his dogs will chase you. They will catch you, cut off your flesh, and boil it. You are brave. Don't be frightened. Before they come, you run around and around the island. Cover your tracks so that the dogs will lose your scent. Then make an image of a man out of stringy wood moss. Put the image in a tree and put a bow and arrow in its hands. Then make other images of men with bows and arrows. After you have put them in many trees, come to me again."

The young man did as he was told. He ran around the island several times. He made the images out of wood moss and put them up in trees. Then he went back to the skeleton. The skeleton said to him, "Hunt up my bow and pipe, take a few whiffs, and hand the pipe to me."

The young man found the bow and pipe. He lit the pipe, took a few whiffs, and handed it to the skeleton. The skeleton took a long pull, and mice ran out of his bones where they had been living. The skeleton felt better when the mice had left. He was able to talk more.

He said, "The man-eater will come to the island in a boat. Before they land, the dogs will quarrel about which will get out first. When they are out, they will follow your scent. At daybreak they will return to the boat. The man-eater will run behind the dogs with a club to drive off the dogs when they catch you.

"The boat is propelled by ducks. The ducks will hunt for

food until they are recalled. You hide yourself in the sand where the boat lands. You will hear everything. Every time a dog touches a tree where there is an image, the image will come to life and will kill the dog with the bow and arrow. All the dogs will be killed. The man-eater will be delayed waiting for his dogs to return to life.

"The man-eater has two women at home who do the cooking for him. When the dogs and the man-eater are following your tracks around the island, jump into the boat. Call the ducks. Sing, 'Now, now, come and propel the boat.' They will come. Go to the man-eater's house. Step lightly on the shore and send the ducks away. In the house of the man-eater, you will find the lower half of my body hanging up over the fireplace. I was master there once. I want you to bring the women here. The man-eater will find some way to get back to his home."

The young man did as he was told and hid in the sand. He heard the dogs quarreling. He listened while the man and his dogs started to follow his tracks. When they were gone, he crept out of his hiding place in the sand. He jumped into the boat and sang, "Now, now, come and propel the boat. Now, now, come and propel the boat." The ducks came and propelled the boat across the water to the opposite shore. It was a long distance, so it took a long time to get there. He told the ducks not to go too far away. He picked up the boat, carried it under his arm, and walked up to the house. The house was on a knoll not far from the shore.

When one of the girls who lived in the house saw the young man, she called out to him, "It would be better for you to leave! A man-eater lives here. He will eat you up."

The young man answered, "I am here to release you. I have a brother over on the island. Those legs hanging up there over the fireplace are his. I am going to free you and your sister."

The girl went into the house and talked with her sister. She returned after a while and said, "You can't kill the man-eater, but we will protect you against him. We will put you in a hole in the ground in the house, and you must stay there until we call you to come out."

The sisters scraped up all the earth where he had walked so as to destroy his footsteps. They threw the earth into the fire.

When the dogs came to the island they smelled the man's scent, although the girls had been careful. Everywhere about his tracks, the dogs barked at the girls. The girls sent them out of the house. The dogs lay down. Soon they started up again eagerly. The girls scolded them and made them quiet down.

At dark the man-eater returned to the island in another boat. The girls had fed the young man with good food and kept him hidden well. The boy saw the man-eater as he was starting away again. The man-eater was a big, rough-looking man with warts on his face.

When the man-eater was a safe distance away, the young man called to the half-skeleton to come down from the place where it was hanging. It came down. The girls packed up their goods and went to the shore. There were different ducks for the different boats. The girls and the young man sang, "Now, now, come and propel this boat. Now, now, come and propel this boat." The ducks came. The three young people got into the boat and they started for the island.

Very soon one girl cried out, "Look out! Look out!" Right behind them was the man-eater. He had a hook and line. He threw the end with his hook on it, and the hook caught onto the young people's boat. Their boat was drawn straight towards the man-eater. But the young man broke the hook, and he paddled twice as fast as he had before.

Soon the other girl cried, "Look out! Look out!" Just out of reach, the man-eater was behind the young man. He was ready to strike the young man with a hammer. The boy hit the man-eater with a paddle. The man-eater had been drinking seawater. When the paddle struck him, it cut him open and the seawater rushed out. The man-eater reached the shore, but his skin was so stretched that he could not get himself together. The boy tore him to pieces.

When the two girls and the young man reached the half-skeleton on the island, the half-skeleton said to the boy, "You are a brave, noble young man. Now get my pipe and light it for me."

The young man lit the pipe and handed it to the half-skeleton. The skeleton smoked. More mice ran out from his bones. The young man took the lower half of his brother, which he had found in the man-eater's house, and joined it to the half-skeleton. He built a tepee over the two halves. Then he went and cut down a tree so that it fell towards the tepee.

The young man called, "Look out or you will be killed!" and his brother, alive and whole, came out of the tepee.

He said to the young man, "These girls are our sisters. On this island are many more bones which the man-eater did not take home. The other bones are at the man-eater's house. Let us gather all these bones into a heap."

They piled in a heap all the bones on the island. They got the rest of the bones from the man-eater's house and put them on the pile. They built a tepee over the pile of bones. The men burned tobacco. They asked the Great Spirit to give life to the bones. Then they cut a tree so that it fell towards the tepee.

They called, "Look out! Look out! Run or you will be killed."

A great number of people ran out from the tepee in all directions. Then they all went back to the lodge where the boy had once lived under the bed. They found his uncle crying because he thought that the boy had been killed. When he saw the boy, as well as his brother and sisters, he became very happy. He welcomed all the people, and there they all lived together ever after.

CHAPTER EIGHTEEN

Dry Bones in the Sand

As I listened in depth to this story, I found far more than a simple tale of the supernatural. The beach upon which the young man found the bones of his brother has many correspondences with Ezekiel's vision of the Valley of Dry Bones, in Ezekiel 37. The Hebrew prophet's vision spoke not primarily of personal resurrection, but of the transformation and rebirth of the people of Israel. In the midst of despair and exile, the prophet proclaimed that Israel would not be only dry bones, but a living people again. This myth speaks of the continued life of a Native American nation; it will not be blotted out. This nation will live again. The dry bones of the nearly exterminated Seneca and Iroquois will come to life and the nation will continue on, as indeed it has.

The clue to the story is the statement of the uncle that the boy who lived with him was the last one of his tribe. For this reason the uncle employed very harsh measures to keep the boy alive, tying him under the bed with the roots of a tree wrapped around him. The potential hero was restrained by the fear of the uncle that the man-eater who had destroyed all the other members of his people would destroy this youth as well. Could this story arise out of the agony of an oppressed people? The man-eater may well refer to the Europeans who had gobbled up the Native American land and held them in virtual captivity. Like Moses, this potential liberator of his people was hidden away as a child to keep him safe.

In both this myth and that of Ezekiel we find the intimation of personal immortality. Without the idea of human beings rising from the dead, the analogy of the nation being saved made little sense, but this is not the primary thrust of this myth. Unless a people has a sense of destiny, a belief that they can overcome all obstacles, they can be consumed and disappear as completely as if eaten by a man-eater. The visions of Handsome Lake did for the Seneca and their sister nations what the visions and prophecies of the great Hebrew prophets did for the Hebrews. In my lifetime I have seen the dry bones of Israel become a landed nation once again and have also seen the Iroquois issuing their own passports.

The real hero cannot be contained by the collective ideas of the past, those of the uncle. Instead of waiting for the man-eater to find him, the youth set out to find and destroy the one who had annihilated his family and his people. The tragic account of such a lone survivor of a California Native American tribe is found in the book, *Ishi in Two Worlds*, by Theodora Kroeber. Ishi ended his days displaying Stone Age crafts in a San Francisco museum, and with him his people died. Several times the hero of our myth was restrained from action by the clairvoyant songs that came to his uncle while he went about his lonely work. Finally, however, the time was right. No song or intuition came to the uncle and the youth broke free and ventured forth from his prison-home.

He crossed a small stream of water and found an island; but this was a magical island and once the hero was upon it, the island moved away from shore. The youth realized that he could not return and he sat down and moaned. Few heroes or saviors are immediately successful; first they pass through trials and tribulations. Elijah fleeing King Ahab sat down in despair and hopelessness before he went on and heard the still, small voice. Reduced to desperation, the youth was forced to look around him and he saw some bones sticking up out of the sand.

I personally find my most convincing intimations of hope when I have been reduced to despair. I wish it were otherwise, and what is true for me is not true for everyone. I find that a divine savior is waiting to help me when I have no human resource available. I feel that I am alone on a desert island. Isolation and quiet have been age-old preparations for the hero's journey. The island is the perfect symbol for isolation, refuge from the surrounding seas of unconscious confusion, from other people and from collective thinking. Some seek isolation and others have it forced upon them. The hero uses the island of separation for transformation. The holy island of the Greeks, Delos, was also known as the floating island and other floating islands are found in many different mythologies. Allusions to islands as places of recreative transformation and preparation are found in many great works of world literature.

Ezekiel saw dry bones in the desert; the youth found them in the sand by the sea. The sand is what survives when rocky cliffs are reduced to sand by the waves. The sand is the border between the ocean of the unconscious and the solid land. Sand often reveals buried treasures. I have often received important insights while sitting alone on the sand, listening to the pounding waves. The sand of the desert and of the sea have much in common.

When the hero dug around the bones, he found the upper part of a human skeleton and it whispered to him that it was the youth's brother. Then the voice went on to tell him how to escape the man-eater. He was to make magic human effigies of the moss that grows in trees, arm them with bows and arrows, and place them in the trees around the island. The hero was told to hunt for his brother's bow and his pipe which were hidden in the sand. He was instructed to light the pipe and share in the holy ritual of communing with the spirit world. After a long puff of tobacco the skeleton felt much better, and the mice as symbols of death leave his frame. He then described exactly what would happen and what the hero was to do after the enemy was destroyed.

We have not previously encountered in these myths bones that could talk and save the living. Bones have been an important human symbol since the time of the Neanderthals. Careful burials of human skeletons with reddened bones have been discovered that date back fifty thousand years. Bones were seen as the indestructible part of human beings, and so were symbols and carriers of the immortal soul. It was also believed that the bones retained something of the power of the human beings to whom they had belonged. Relics, pieces of bone or skin, of holy people have been kept in churches or by individuals so they could share in the holiness that still clung to them. Relics of the recently sainted Mother Seton were available at the mother house of her order. Both animal and human bones have been used in healing charms, spells, and divination. The skeleton has often been displayed to induce awe and fear as a symbol of the mystery of death and of the uncanny realm beyond death.

Everything in our story worked out as the bones had foretold. After hiding in the sand, the hero used his godlike shamanistic powers and took possession of the boat propelled by the ducks, whom we have met before: the animals who can live in air, on the ground, or under the water. He ordered the ducks to take him to the home of the man-eater. There he found the two women who took care of the man-eater. They warned him to leave. The youth ignored their warning and told them that he had come to free them from their bondage. The sisters told him that he could not kill the man-eater, but they would hide him from his enemy. They even scraped up the dirt where he had stepped and threw the dirt into the fire, so the bloodhound-like dogs could not follow his scent. After feeding him well they hid him in a hole in the floor. The man-eater and his dogs returned and, although the dogs barked, the sisters quieted them and the man-eater did not suspect an intruder.

The next morning as the man and his dogs left the cabin, the youth caught a glimpse of the man-eater; he was big, rough-looking, and had warts on his face. In our first story the man-eater had warts on his face that disappeared when he changed his ways. In the folklore of many different cultures warts are associated with the devil and with witches who use spiritual power for evil. They have even been seen as teats from which familiar spirits could suck their sustenance. Thus, getting rid of warts was of the greatest importance.

I was brought up in rural Pennsylvania where the hex doctors prescribed different rituals for getting rid of warts. One consisted of tossing smooth pebbles over the left shoulder at the time of the new moon. These cures often worked; modern studies using the double blind test have shown that suggestion can remove most warts nearly as successfully as surgery. In one instance a young man with persistent warts was diagnosed by his doctor as having great guilt. When he dealt with his guilt his warts disappeared. Witches and man-eaters may have had more guilt than they realized.

When the man-eater was safely on his way, the youth-shaman called for the half-skeleton to come down from the place where it hung. With the two women they went to a boat and called the ducks to come to their help. In this crisis both the women and the youth sang their magic song. As in movies of pursuit, the witch-man-eater was soon after them. After near disaster, the hero struck the monster with a paddle. The man-eater split open and seawater rushed out. The youth then tore him to pieces. This creature had lived on the water of the sea, the great unconscious, and when struck by the paddle he simply split apart. The paddle was the instrument that enabled the Seneca to get around their well-watered land. It was a symbol of consciously directed energy, a rudder and a sail at the same time. The monster was unable to deal with consciousness and was torn apart. The paddle was also used to strike people running the gauntlet, as we have seen in other tales, and is still used in initiations in many fraternities today, a symbol of power and submission to power.

The skeleton brother was then reassembled. The skeleton smoked and more mice scurried away. Once again the survivors built a tepee over the skeleton and cut a tree to fall toward it. I need to remind myself again and again that it was the life-giving world tree falling through a hole in the sky that made possible the creation of the earth in the first place. Then I truly begin to see the subtle significance of the falling tree. As the tree fell towards the tepee, the youth called a warning to flee and the brother emerged alive and well. The resurrected one then told his brother that the women were their sisters.

The bones of their tribe littered the island and the space around the man-eater's house. The four of them collected all the bones they could find and placed them in a great pile, then built a great tepee over them. Then we hear these significant words, "The men burned tobacco. They asked the Great Spirit to give life to the bones." They prayed, they opened themselves to the divine in the best way that they knew, and they repeated the ritual of the falling tree. A great number of their people came running out of the tepee.

The nation, the tribe, the people were alive again. The two brothers and two sisters went back to the lodge where the boy had lived under the bed. Their coming dried the tears of the uncle who thought his nephew had been killed, and they all lived on together ever after. The hero had won the battle and harmony was established once again. His people lived again. There is hope in spite of the man-eaters and evil that surround us.

CHAPTER NINETEEN

Sore Legs

Do-nyo-sa-we-oh was a young man. He lived with his grand-mother. One day his grandmother said, "You are old enough to have a wife now. Go to the house across the field. A widow lives there. She has ten daughters. You go this evening and get acquainted with the oldest daughter. You must ask her mother if you may talk with the girl. Then she will know you are looking for a wife. She will know you have chosen the oldest daughter."

Do-nyo-sa-we-oh was bashful. He did not know women. He did not know how to act with them. He did not wish to go to the home of the widow woman. He decided that he would find out which one of the daughters would make the best wife. He dressed himself in a bearskin. This still had oil in it and was cleaned so as to leave what looked like scars. The bearskin fitted Do-nyo-sa-we-oh so closely that it did not look as though he had bearskin on his legs. It looked as though he had sore legs.

Towards evening Do-nyo-sa-we-oh started for the widow's house. He reached the house, but he did not dare to knock or speak or show he was there. It was very dark. He stood on the threshold. He leaned against one doorpost with a foot against the opposite post. By blocking the way, he could tell if anyone came out of the house.

Finally, during the night, the widow came through the door. She tumbled over his leg.

Do-nyo-sa-we-oh cried, "Oh! You hurt my leg. You hurt my leg."

She said, "Why are you here?"

He said, "My grandmother sent me over to get your oldest daughter to be my wife."

She said, "You had better come in the house. We will talk matters over by daylight." She made a bed for him. All the daughters were asleep.

In the morning the mother and girls prepared breakfast. They roasted white corn. When it was brown, they put the corn in a pounder and pounded the corn with a stick. When it was ground, they divided it equally among the family and guest. Each one fixed it the way he or she liked best. Some ate it just as it was, some with sugar, and others with maple molasses.

They gave a dish of the corn flour to Do-nyo-sa-we-oh. He put the dish on the ground near the fire. He picked what seemed to be scabs off his sore legs. He squeezed the bearskin so that the oil ran into the dish of meal. He stirred it up and ate it. He acted as though he liked it very much. The women were disgusted. They thought that Do-nyo-sa-we-oh really had sore legs. He asked the oldest daughter to come and eat with him.

The oldest daughter said, "No." She ate her own share of cornmeal.

After they had eaten, the mother said to her oldest daughter, "What are you going to do? This young man comes to ask you to be his wife."

The daughter said, "I will not be his wife. I would not have such a man for my husband."

The old woman said to Do-nyo-sa-we-oh, "You hear what my daughter says. That is the end of it."

The young man, very lame, limped home. His grandmother asked him about his luck. He said, "I had bad luck. No one will have me for a husband. The oldest daughter did not like me."

The grandmother answered, "You go there again tomorrow night. There are nine more girls for you to ask to live with you."

The next night Do-nyo-sa-we-oh went to the home of the widow. He did not knock or let them know that he was there. He stood on the threshold. He leaned against one doorpost with his foot on the opposite doorpost. Finally, the old woman came out of the house. She tripped over his leg, so that he fell down.

He cried, "Oh! You hurt my leg. You hurt my leg."

She said, "Why are you here?"

He answered, "My grandmother sent me over to ask the next oldest daughter if she will be my wife."

She said, "We will talk this over by daylight." She made a bed for him. The daughters were asleep.

In the morning the old woman and her daughters prepared breakfast. They ground squaw corn and divided it. Each one fixed her own share as she wished. Do-nyo-sa-we-oh fixed his corn as he had done the morning before. The girls watched him closely.

The next to the oldest daughter said, "I don't want to be his wife. He is a sick man with sores all over his body." She went out of the house and the young man went home.

Each night after that he returned and had the same experiences. At last only the youngest daughter was left. The mother had more control over this daughter than she had over the other daughters. The mother talked to the youngest daughter and said, "I am sure that Do-nyo-sa-we-oh is not a sick man. He is well and well-to-do. I advise you to eat with him in the morning."

That night the young man came. He did not knock or let the people know he was there. He stood on the threshold. He leaned against one doorpost with his foot against the opposite post. Finally, the mother of the daughters came out of the house. She fell over his leg and knocked him over.

He cried, "Oh! You hurt my leg. You hurt my leg."

She said, "Why are you here?"

He answered, "My grandmother sent me over here to ask your youngest daughter to be my wife."

The mother said, "We will talk this over by daylight." She made a bed for him and he slept.

In the morning, the mother and her ten daughters prepared the corn. Some ate it with sugar, some with maple molasses, and some with meat broth. Do-nyo-sa-we-oh fixed his corn as he had done each morning before. The women would hear him grind the scabs with his teeth as he ate. He asked the youngest girl to eat with him. She ate.

She said, "Oh! How good it is." She ate so much of it that he had only a little breakfast. The mother said to the girl, "Do-nyo-sa-we-oh is to be your husband. You are to live with him." The mother and daughter prepared the wedding cakes. These were made of corn and boiled in the husks. They all ate together. Do-nyo-sa-we-oh and the youngest girl were man and wife.

The mother said, "You may make your home here."

The young man took the bearskin off and hung it up. Then the women knew that the scabs and sores were only bear grease which he had squeezed into the corn.

Do-nyo-sa-we-oh said to his wife, "We must live by ourselves. We will go into the woods and build a home."

They gathered provisions together. They put clothes and skins on their backs and started for the woods. In the woods, he built a log house with the fire in the middle of the room and a hole in the roof instead of a chimney.

When it was finished, Do-nyo-sa-we-oh said to his wife, "We must have some meat. I have a magic way of bringing animals to the house. You lie down in back of the door. I will cover you up with a skin. You must not look out while I am getting game."

She lay down and he covered her up with a skin. He went outdoors. Just outside the door, he began singing, "All animals take a journey! Start now and come here! All animals take a journey! Start now and come here!"

All at once the wife could hear a rumbling outdoors. All kinds of animals flocked to the yard. Do-nyo-sa-we-oh shot and killed many animals. His wife could hear the bow string each time he shot. When he had killed all the animals he wished for, he came into the house and uncovered his wife. They took care of the game. There were all kinds, deer, bear, and elk. They had a great amount of meat. They hung up the skins and meat to dry.

When it was all cared for, Do-nyo-sa-we-oh sent his wife to her mother's and to his grandmother's to invite both families to come after meat. The mother, sisters, and grandmother came to the log house in the woods and took home with them all the meat they could carry. It was a long time before they were in need of meat again.

Several weeks later, Do-nyo-sa-we-oh told his wife that he

was going to kill more game. She lay down behind the door. He covered her up with a skin. He went outside of the house. Just beyond the door he began to sing, "All animals take a journey! Start now and come here! All animals take a journey! Start now and come here!"

The wife could hear the rumbling in the yard. All kinds of animals came. Do-nyo-sa-we-oh shot many bears and deer. He went into the house, uncovered his wife, and said, "Help me take care of the meat." They lived happily and had plenty to eat.

They were there for nearly a year and they were happy together in the woods. One day he told her to lie down behind the door and not to look outdoors. He covered her with a blanket of skin and went out of the house. Just outside, he began to sing, "Gar-yeh-heh, Gar-yeh-heh. All animals make a journey! Start now and come here! All animals make a journey! Start now and come here!"

The animals flocked into the yard. The wife did not obey her husband. She looked out. Just as she looked, a great elk hooked her husband and ran off with him. Then she cried because she had been so foolish. She wished that she had obeyed her husband. After he was taken away by the elk, she could hear him singing, farther and farther away in the distance, the same song, "Gar-yeh-heh, Gar-yeh-heh." In the afternoon she packed up her things and went back to her mother's home.

Her mother and sisters asked, "Where is your husband?"

She answered, "I disobeyed my husband. I looked out when he was getting game. I saw a great elk hook him and carry him away." She mourned deeply for her husband. Her mother and sisters were sorry for her and mourned with her. The next day her sisters went to the log house in the woods and brought what she had left of meat and goods to their mother's house. The grandmother of Do-nyo-a-we-oh was told what had happened to her grandson.

The old woman moaned and said, "I was afraid that would happen to my grandson. I was afraid she would disobey."

After a while the wife of Do-nyo-sa-we-oh had a child. It was a boy. Each day, early in the morning she went outdoors. Far away in the distance, she could hear a faint sound. It was

the voice of her husband. It sang, "Gar-yeh-heh, Gar-yeh-heh."
Every day since he had left, wherever the elk was carrying him,
she could hear the singing, "Gar-yeh-heh" very high, like an
echo. The baby boy grew old enough to play outdoors. When
he was old enough to play with other boys he heard the boys
say, "Father." He came to his mother.

He said, "What do the boys mean by 'Father'?"

His mother said to him, "You are fortunate. You have had a
father, but I suppose your father is dead. We had a house in the
woods. We lived happily there. He had a magic way of getting
game. He told me I must not look. I disobeyed and looked. A
great elk carried him away on his horns. I left our home, which
is back in the woods, to live here with my mother. You get up
early in the morning about daylight and go outdoors. You will
hear singing. You will know that it is your father."

He arose the next morning and went outdoors early. He could
hear a faint song, "Gar-yeh-heh!" and then the echo, "Gar-yeh-
heh. All animals make a journey! Start now and come here! All
animals make a journey! Start now and come here!" He listened
fully. Then the boy went in the house and sang the song for
his mother.

His mother said, "Yes, that is your father singing."

The boy said, "I think I had better go to our home in the
woods. I can hunt as well as my father did." They talked about
it, and they decided to go. So they gathered up their things and
started for the log house in the woods.

It was nearly a day's journey to the house. When they reached
the house, they built a fire and settled there. When it was done,
the boy said to his mother, "Tell me just how father killed the
game." She told him that his father had her lie down and then
he covered her up and told her not to look. She said that when
he was just outside the house, he sang, "All the animals make
a journey! Start now and come here!" She taught the song to
the boy.

He said, "We will get up early in the morning and do as
father did."

The father had left an extra bow and arrow hanging up on
the log wall. The boy's mother gave them to the boy. The next
morning the boy told his mother to lie down and he covered

her with a skin blanket. He went outdoors and sang, "Gar-yeh-heh. All animals make a journey! Start now and come here! All animals make a journey! Start now and come here!"

There was a great rumbling. All kinds of animals flocked to the yard. The boy saw a great elk with bones hanging on its horns. He shot this elk, but killed nothing else. He showed his mother the great elk that had carried away his father. The boy carefully took his father's bones off the elk's horns. He carried them quite a long way from the house. He put the head towards the east, as the Seneca bury their dead. He built a tepee over his father's bones, after he had straightened them out carefully. The boy kicked down a big hickory tree which fell towards the tepee.

The boy called, "Father! Come out or the tree will fall on you."

The boy saw his father spring to life and jump aside, and the tree fell just where his father had lain. The mother was very happy to see her husband. She took him into the house. The next day they went to her mother's home. He looked as though nothing had happened to him.

Her mother said, "You might as well stay here."

So they brought his grandmother there and all lived together. When they wanted meat or furs, Do-nyo-sa-we-oh went to the log house in the woods. They always had plenty of meat, for he kept his magic power.

CHAPTER TWENTY

A Happy Ending

In the first legend, a magical father is saved by an even more magical son. The same theme runs through the remarkable story of Haton-dos. In the final, dream-like tale, a magical father is resurrected by his magical son. It is interesting to note that in each of these myths only the fathers are given names; the sons remain nameless.

Do-nyo-sa-we-oh was a young man living with his grandmother. We are not told what happened to his mother or father or uncle. In a matrilineal society, the grandmother raised a child if the other relatives had been killed in war, taken prisoner, or died. The fact that no special note is made about this living situation suggests that it was not unusual.

The grandmother is a significant archetypal image. The grandmother is the positive side of the Great Mother, the representative of the Great Mother Goddess that dominated human culture from the beginning of civilization, (which was largely a feminine creation). Most advances in civilization and culture were feminine creations, then men began to use their weapons to seize the wealth accumulated by women of other villages. At the same time, women became servants (or slaves) of men and patriarchy was born. This transformation of society took place only six or seven thousand years ago. The Iroquois (and some other Native American nations) were one of the few peoples to make the transition from matrilineal society without devaluing women.

The hero was raised by a wise Great Mother and he was well acquainted with women's mysteries as well as with the skills of the hunter-warrior. His magical powers came from the union of these two gifts. Few men know the reality of the spiritual world and how to deal with it unless they can relate to the powerful Great Mother archetype within and beyond the human soul. In Christian society, the veneration of the Virgin Mother as maiden, mother, wife, and *pietà* (guiding her son through death) provided contact with this deep aspect of the Holy. Often in dreams the grandmother has this archetypal significance.

This wise woman knew that her bashful charge needed to have contact with the outer feminine if he was to be in touch with his inner feminine and become a mature, whole person. There was little reticence on sexual matters among the Seneca. She simply told him, "It is time for you to take a wife. There is a widow across the field with ten daughters. Go and marry one." Do-nyo-sa-we-oh didn't want to go, but the Great Mother had spoken. It may be the Great Mother speaking that forces many young men into marriage even today. The hero didn't know how to deal with women and he wanted to find the right one, one who would be willing to take him just as he was. His ruse was clever: he dressed in a bearskin with the fur side clipped and worn against his skin. The raw side with bubbles of bear fat on it was thus on the outside and it made him look as though he had sore legs. Only a person of power could have created such a perfect disguise.

The young man was too bashful to knock on the door and so he leaned against the doorpost with his leg across the doorway. During the night the widow came out and stumbled over his leg. When she asked why he was there, the youth blurted out that he had come to take one of her daughters for a wife. He was invited in and so gained entrance to the house. The Seneca who heard the tale were probably as amused by this archetypal adolescent male as we are today when the figure appears in movies or cartoons.

We must imagine ourselves in a Seneca longhouse in order to get the full humor of the story. Humor is a marvelous way to gain attention for a serious story. In the morning when all those in the longhouse were awake, a breakfast of cornmeal mush was served. Some of them ate it with maple sugar, others with maple syrup, but the hero picked what appeared to be a scab on his sore legs and squeezed its contents on his mush. Naturally the oldest daughter was disgusted and wanted nothing to do with the strange young man. The relieved youth went home and told his grandmother no one wanted him. Then in authentic slapstick comedy, the same situation is repeated eight more times: the grandmother sends the youth back, the widow woman falls over the youth's leg in the doorway, the young man displays his disgusting eating habits, he is rejected and returns home.

The widow woman was astute and saw through the ruse, and having more control over the youngest daughter, the most pliable and agreeable, she convinced the girl that the suitor was not only healthy, but also well-to-do. The youth returned and invited her to taste his cereal seasoned with bear fat. She did so and found it so delicious that she left little for the young man. The youngest daughter is an archetypal symbol for the adaptable and malleable aspect of the feminine depicted in the Chinese book of wisdom, the *I Ching*, as well as in many folktales.

The mother then proclaimed there would be a wedding and told the youngest daughter, "He will be your husband. You will live with him." Then the sacramental wedding cakes were made of the corn that sprang from the breasts of the divine Earth Mother. They all ate the cakes together and the marriage ceremony was complete. Only then did Do-nyo-sa-we-oh take off his bear skin and reveal what a handsome youth he really was.

The groom and his bride then went off to make a life for themselves. He built a log cabin with a fire hole in the roof and they put away all the possessions they had brought with them. Do-nyo-sa-we-oh revealed that he was a magic hunter. He told his wife that she must lie down and be covered with an animal skin. His magic had power only if his wife was kept hidden and did not watch him. There was a masculine mystique as well as a feminine one and each was sacred.

At first the wife was obedient when the young man called, "Gar-yeh-heh, Gar-yeh-heh," and commanded all the animals to come to him at his log home. They came as a thundering herd and he killed all the game that they, her mother, and his grandmother could use. This ritual was repeated whenever they needed meat. They lived happily together for nearly a year.

Then one day the bride became curious and as all the animals came running to obey the call, she threw off the skin and looked out at her husband. At that very moment a great elk hooked her husband on its horns and carried him away. Her paradise was lost.

Disobedience causing disaster and bringing an end to the happy, carefree life is a recurring theme in religion and mythology. Adam and Eve disobeyed and were driven out of the garden. Psyche lived in perfect bliss with Cupid (Eros) in their nighttime encounters until she became curious and disobeyed him. She lighted a lamp to behold her lover, she saw his beauty, and then her heaven vanished. Psyche had to perform many tasks and suffer great agony before paradise was regained. The hero's wife could still hear in the distance the song her husband had sung to bring the game. Brokenhearted because of her foolishness and loss, she packed up her things and went home.

Up to this point the deer and elk have merely been seen as necessary meat for the people of our legends, but now the elk assumes another meaning as it carries away the husband of the disobedient wife. The stag, the deer, and the elk are interrelated symbols. The stag and elk are noble animals, king-like. In mythology, Actaeon was turned into a stag when he stumbled on Diana bathing. The elk sheds its horns; these horns became symbols of immortality. One large, fraternal association is known as the Beneficent and Protective Order of Elks. The elk has been seen as a fertility symbol in many cultures. The elk is almost a totem for Canada as the eagle is for the United States. The noblest and most powerful of the deer family carried away her husband when curiosity sought to understand the magic of the hunt and masculinity. Pure curiosity can destroy the mystery and power of the masculine. And yet, the husband's song still reverberated through the forest and at times she could hear it dimly in the distance.

Then a son was born, a savior. To those who know the Christian Christmas story, the very words sound familiar. The son grew up knowing nothing of his father, not even what the word "father" meant. When the boy asked his mother about his father, she told him the whole story, honestly. His mother never denied her guilt — very different from Eve.

The boy got up early in the morning and heard the faint song that his father had sung still echoing in the forest. The boy then took charge of his mother and told her they would go to their former home, a day's journey from where they now lived. When they arrived at the lodge his father had built, he found a bow and arrow. His mother taught him his father's hunting-medicine song. The mother was covered up and the boy sang the song and his power was the same as his father's.

Among the animals that flocked around the log cabin was a huge elk with the skeleton of his father hanging from the antlers. The boy killed only the elk. In characteristic Seneca fashion, he treated these bones with great respect and carried them a long way from the lodge. He laid them out with the head pointing to the east as the Iroquois bury their dead. He built a tepee over the bones and kicked down a big hickory tree. He called to his father to escape from the falling tree. His father sprang to life and jumped aside. Paradise was regained. Do-nyo-sa-we-oh and his wife were happily rejoined, and the grandmother was invited to come and live with them. When the family needed meat the hero-father went to the lodge alone and used his hunting magic, and so he avoided further disaster.

We see here a picture of the fall, the birth of a savior, the redemption of the fall, and the resurrection of the one whom evil curiosity had destroyed. This tale, like so many others, brings us back to the harmony of the strawberry road.

Epilogue

And what do these tales tell us about maturity and fulfilment of our human existence, about the way of the hero? They tell us that achieving a satisfactory life is a long and arduous task and requires more than merely human effort. They tell us that there is evil in the world and we have to face it and deal with it. To do this we need supernatural help.

They speak of the union of the masculine and the feminine. Men and women need to know and relate with each other in the outer world to achieve maturity. In addition, women need to connect with their inner masculine and men with their inner feminine. Whole human beings have accomplished the holy inner marriage.

Age and power are not enough. Age needs to be rejuvenated by youth, by its vigor, creativity, and flexibility. Youth requires the guidance and direction, the wisdom and knowledge that age and experience alone can provide. Plato, in the *Laws*, writes that no legislator may sit in the legislative assembly unless accompanied by a youth. Age and youth need each other.

These tales again reaffirm the importance of hope. If we do not hope we are usually lost and we seldom come to wholeness. Beyond the seen world is the unseen that touches and empowers it. At death we enter fully into the beyond.

Courage and persistence are required of all heroes whether they are on the outer journey or the inner one. Indeed, these two journeys are inseparable.

Although little is said about love and kindness, they are

implied. Unless there is love and forebearance, masculine and feminine cannot have harmony between them. Youth and age need to respect, understand, and work with one another, if they are to learn how to be flexible, creative, stable, and wise.

Last of all, these tales portray the world as a good place and the universe as one that is essentially directed toward peace and harmony. With Mother Julian they sing the theme: And all will be well. And all will be well.

Notes

CHAPTER ONE

1. The version that I follow is one that has been summarized in *The Death and Rebirth of the Seneca* (New York: Random House Inc., 1972), pp. 85–92. Anthony F. C. Wallace has drawn from the best historical sources available, and documented his sources carefully in his footnotes. The reader who wishes a more detailed account can consult Wallace and his sources. A Mohawk version is given in *National Geographic*, Vol. 180, No. 4, Oct. 1991, pp. 72–76.
2. I have discussed this whole matter at length in my book, *God, Dreams and Revelation* (Minneapolis: Augsburg Fortress, 1991).
3. I have examined this almost unbelievable phenomenon in Chapter Four, The Patriarchal Putdown, in a book my wife and I wrote entitled, *Sacrament of Sexuality* (Rockport, MA: Element Books, 1991).
4. A fine imaginative account of a Mohawk village in 1491 was written by Joseph Bruchac in *National Geographic*, Vol. 180, No. 4, Oct. 1991, pp. 68–82. Life among the Seneca would have been somewhat similar.

CHAPTER FIVE

1. An interesting commentary on the white stone is found in F. Aster Barnwell's *Meditations on the Apocalypse* (Rockport, MA: Element Books, 1992) pp. 153–154.

CHAPTER ELEVEN

1. In my book, *Christianity as Psychology* (Minneapolis: Augsburg Fortness, 1984), I have referred to the work of several authorities on missionary work who take seriously this intermediate spiritual realm. They state that Jesus and the New Testament speak of this realm. They suggest that many missionary programs are more interested in Westernizing converts to Christianity than in Christ-ianizing them. In *Discernment: A Study in Ecstasy and Evil* (Mahwah, NJ: Paulist Press, 1978), I have discussed the nature of this realm at length.

CHAPTER THIRTEEN

1. I have discussed this symbol at length in *Myth, History and Faith* (Rockport, MA: Element Books, 1991).

Recommended Reading

For those who wish to study more about the myths, symbols, and images of the Native Americans and about the same images that arise in all of us, we have listed below two quite different kinds of material. One refers to the Native Americans with particular emphasis on the Iroquois. The other deals with the vast subject of symbols and their archetypal meanings.

NATIVE AMERICAN STUDIES

Huston Smith's newly revised and updated, *The World's Religions* (San Francisco: HarperCollins, 1991) gives a magnificent overview of the human religious search. Chapter IX of this book provides the finest study of the religion of those who had not yet committed their practices to writing.

Black Elk Speaks, by John G. Neihardt (Lincoln, Nebraska: University of Nebraska Press, 1979) first awakened me to the religious tradition of Native Americans. Carl Jung stated that it was one of the finest examples of the religious depth of the unconscious.

Then I discovered Mircea Eliade's exhaustive studies of religious experience in his book *Shamanism* (Princeton: Princeton University Press, 1970). This book made a deep impression on my students at Notre Dame and is a must for those who would understand the nature of religious experience and Native American religion in particular.

Some of the books that have made a great impression on me are: Andrew Weil, *The Natural Mind* (Boston: Houghton Mifflin, 1972); Joseph Epes Brown, *The Sacred Pipe* (Norman, OK: University of

Oklahoma Press, 1989); Theodora Kroeber, *Ishi in Two Worlds* (Berkeley: University of California Press, 1976), a biography of the last wild Native American in North America; Franc Johnson Newcomb, *Hosteen Klah: Navaho Medicine Man and Sand Painter* (Norman, OK: University of Oklahoma Press, 1972); David Villasenor, *Tapestries in Sand: The Spirit of Indian Sandpainting* (Healdsburg, CA: Naturegraph Company, 1966); F. Bruce Lamb, *Wizard of the Upper Amazon* (Boston: Houghton Mifflin, 1975); M. Vera Buhrmann, *Living in Two Worlds: Communications Between a White Healer and Her Black Counterparts* (Cape Town: Human & Rousseau, 1984).

Several general books on Native Americans have been helpful to me: Peter Farb, *Man's Rise to Civilization: As Shown by the Indians of North America from Primeval Times to the Coming of the Industrial State* (New York: E. P. Dutton, 1968); *Native North American Spirituality of the Eastern Woodlands*, edited by Elizabeth Tooker (New York: Paulist Press, 1979); Paul A. W. Wallace, *Indians in Pennsylvania* (Harrisburg: The Pennsylvania Historical and Museum Commission, 1991); *The World of the American Indian*, edited by Jules B. Billard (Washington, D.C.: National Geographic Society, 1974); *National Geographic*, Oct. 1991, Vol. 180, No. 4, is largely devoted to Native American culture, and Sept. 1987, Vol. 172, No. 3 gives a picture of the vitality of modern Iroquois life.

My first introduction to the history of the Iroquois was a privately printed booklet by my grandmother, Sarah L. Trippe, *Early History of the Six Nations* with a sketch of the life of Morton Fitch Trippe and his work among the Seneca appended to it, published in 1929. Another privately printed book was written by Charles Congdon in 1967, entitled *Allegany Oxbow, A History of the Allegany State Park and the Allegany Reserve of the Seneca Nation*. This contains personal reflections of an attorney who lived in or around the Allegany Reservation for ninety years and gives accounts of Seneca customs described by many of the Seneca leaders. The finest study of Seneca history and culture is Anthony F. C. Wallace's *The Death and Rebirth of the Seneca* (New York: Random House, Inc., 1972). A history of the Seneca Nation from their point of view is written by George H. J. Abrams, *The Seneca People* (Phoenix, Arizona: Indian Tribal Series, 1976). For the reader interested in the actual content of Handsome Lake's visions and other important Seneca documents, the best book is *Parker on the Iroquois*, edited by William N. Fenton (Syracuse, N.Y.: Syracuse University Press, 1968). In *One More Story* by DuWayne Bowen, (Greenville Center, N.Y.: Bowman Books, 1991) a modern Seneca tells stories of the supernatural that have the same flavor as the tales taken down by my mother in 1901.

An excellent video on the dispute between the Seneca Nation and the City of Salamanca (situated on reservation lands) is *Honorable Nation*, produced by Chana Gazit and David Steward (New Video Group, 419 Park Ave. South, New York, N.Y. 10016, 1991).

Other helpful books are: Donald A. Grinde, Jr., *The Iroquois and the Founding of the American Nation* (The Indian Historian Press, 1977).

Joseph Bruchac, *The Good Message of Handsome Lake* (Greensboro: Unicorn Press, 1979).

W. De Loss Love, *Samson Occom and the Christian Indians of New England* (Boston: Pilgrim Press, 1890).

Henry Lewis Morgan, *League of the Iroquois* (New York: Corinth Books, 1962), a reprint of the classic that appeared in 1851.

SYMBOLOGY

How does one understand and interpret symbols, myths, and dreams? First of all, a wide reading in fairytales and mythology is helpful. I was quite surprised to find the similarity between Asian and European mythological symbols and those found in these Seneca legends. Alexander S. Murray, *Manual of Mythology* (New York: Tudor Publishing Company, 1954) is a good summary of European mythology.

I have already expressed appreciation for Ad de Vries, *Dictionary of Symbols and Imagery* (New York: Elsevier Science Publishing Company, 1984). It is the only dictionary I have encountered that does justice to the symbols with which it deals. It was an invaluable help in opening my understanding to the multitude of meanings found in nearly every symbol.

The Collected Works of C. G. Jung (Princeton: Princeton University Press, various dates) are a mine of wisdom on the meaning of human symbols. Volume 20, the *General Index* to the other nineteen volumes, lists every symbol or image discussed. Jung's autobiography *Memories, Dreams, Reflections*, is excluded from publication in the collected works according to Jung's Last Will and Testament and is an invaluable source for understanding his symbols and dreams. It is also published by Princeton University Press.

Marie-Louise von Franz has written widely on the subject of fairytales and their imagery. Her books, *The Interpretation of Fairytales* and *Problems of the Feminine in Fairytales*, are published by Spring Publications, Irving, Texas.